THE SLEEPING GIANT
THE CHURCH,
ARISE AND SHINE AND TAKE
YOUR RIGHTFUL PLACE

(Faith, Race and Politics Seen Through The Eyes Of A Believer)

SIRENA CHASTANG

Dedication

This book is dedicated in loving memory to the woman that was full of love, compassion and the wisdom of God, my mother Audrey C. Harper, better known as (The Miracle Child). She taught me how to hold on to my faith during the storms of life. Acknowledgments

Thank you, Heavenly Father, for giving me the courage to share my thoughts and feelings and your word, in the hope that this book will bring change to the lives of others.

I would like to thank my husband, Donald, for loving me and supporting me in everything that I do. I love you so much.

Thanks to my beautiful, loving children, Dontae, Briahna, and Tre for always standing by my side.

Thanks to my beloved brother, Chris, and his beautiful daughter, Emily, who brings me great joy.

Thanks to my aunts for always encouraging me.

In loving memory of Gale Banks, a powerful woman of God that was so full of the love of God. Thanks to my prayer partners, Malina, Cathy, Melody, Sharon, and Doris, who are powerful, loving women of God. I thank you for your encouragement, love, support and prayers. Thanks to my pastors that have been instrumental in my life.

Contents

Introduction

The events that have occurred over the last several years, and the love that I have for God's church, moved me to write this book. That love that lives within me, yes, it is a love that comes from Jesus Christ. After the 2016 election, I began to write about everything that I was seeing and feeling about events occurring in our country—writing was therapeutic for me. I wanted to share my perspective on world events, and some of my experiences with the church. We can never know the depth of Christ's love for his church—a church that he sacrificed his only son for, so we could be redeemed. The people of God must stay alert to the enemy's tactics to distract, divide and conquer. The enemy plays on our fears, differences and our selfish tendencies; this book will take you on a journey and prayerfully will aid in leading you to a point of self-reflection. I pray that it will lead whoever God is drawing to reexamine the essence of your walk with Jesus Christ, and lead you to think about your own soul salvation. I wanted to give the reader my insight on the challenges we face as a country and in the church. Yes, the church does have challenges that need to be faced head-on, and I believe if we open our eyes and ears to the truth, and allow God to redirect us and keep us on the right path, then nothing will divide his church again. We are stronger when we are unified. I pray this book will bless and encourage the reader to develop a closer relationship with Jesus Christ, and continue to press forward. I often ask God during my prayer time to keep my heart from turning to stone because of all the trouble and hardships that I see in the world. How we treat each other is enough to keep the strongest individuals in despair. The cowardly, racist rhetoric that some people post on social media to hurt others is so destructive to the soul.

Jeremiah 17:9-10 teaches us, "The heart (is) deceitful above all (things), and desperately wicked: who can know it? I, the Lord, search the heart, I try the reins, even to give every man according to his ways and according to the fruit of his doings."

Psalms 51:10 "Create in me a clean heart, O God; and renew a right spirit within me. Dear Lord, I pray that whomever reads this book will receive and be enlightened by your truth, and they will be in perfect peace. In Jesus' Name, I pray, Amen.

CHAPTER 1

A new era

November 08, 2016, was possibly one of the most shocking days in American history for over half of the country. Yes, this was the day the 45th President of the United States was elected to the highest office in the land. We saw tears and anguish on the faces of many Americans from all walks of life, and at the same time, we saw jubilation from many other Americans. This election was much more than Republicans Versus Democrats; it was more about the state of the country and how divided this nation really is and how we are going in the reverse, as far as race relations are concerned. I know you may be thinking this is nothing new; this country has dealt with racial divides for many years. But something is different now—there has been a shift of great magnitude after one of the most controversial elections that I have ever witnessed. When I officially heard the results the next morning, I felt like someone had knocked the wind out of me. I had a million thoughts running through my mind, but the most significant was the thought of my twelve-year-old son stopping by my room for our morning prayer, just like he does every morning before heading out to the bus stop. Panic overtook my mind for a quick second. I thought to myself: what do I tell him? Lord, help me and give me the words. I don't know what to say—how do I explain this result?

I knew he was going to ask me what had happened, so I quickly gathered myself together and prayed to God to give me the words, even though I was at a loss for words and had no idea what I would tell the child I wanted so much to protect. I looked up at the clock. I knew I would hear the sound of that knock at my door any moment now, so I continued to pray that God would give me the right words to say. I wanted to give him the truth but I did not want to crush his hopes and dreams for a better tomorrow. I did not want my words to tarnish the image of our country. I wondered how I would complete this huge task. The moment had arrived, and I heard a knock at my door. I then raised my head from my pillow, and glanced at those bright eyes filled with so much confusion, and he asked, "How did he win?" I told him there are people hurting and struggling to make it, and they wanted change. So they voted for a dramatic change. And so, whether we believe that this is the change the country needs or not, we have to accept the result, and pray he makes the right decisions for the entire country. I could tell he was still in shock, and he just did not understand the result, after everything that had happened before the election that had hurt and offended so many people from all walks of life.

I wonder if as a nation, we are teaching our children that we can behave badly on so many levels without facing consequences for our actions. When I was a child, my mother taught me there were consequences for bad behavior, and we were to respect and treat people with dignity, regardless of race, creed or color. I tried to pass those same values down to my children.

I have two sons and one daughter, and I have always instilled in them that they have to be respectful, especially when it comes to my sons and them respecting women of all ages. So it was no wonder that my twelve-year-old son was confused by the results of the election. I had many concerns with the outcome of the election but the most troubling concern for the country was the rift that already existed in this country before the election. It was at a six on the Richter scale, if I were to compare it to an earthquake, but the divide after the election is now at an eight, which is considered a 'disaster'. It is heading towards a nine or greater, which is considered on the verge of 'catastrophic'. The definition of 'catastrophic' is 'of the nature of a catastrophe, or disastrous event; calamitous. I know some people may say I am being dramatic. But if people would just stop and look at all the things that are going on in this country, every person of faith would start praying without ceasing. According to a *New York Times* article I read, eighty percent of white evangelicals voted their core principles; they voted based on biblical principles, and that was a vote for the President elect. Some of those same voters believe that the election of the President Elect was the result of a Divine Intervention that assisted him in victory.

One of the prominent pastors from one of our Mega churches said she prayed and fasted and her prayers were answered. She also went on a Christian television network some months after the election to compare the President to a King, and said that anybody going up against him was going against the hand of God. "Because God says that he raises up and places all people in places of authority, it is God who raises up a King. It is God that sets one down.

When you fight against the plan of God, you are fighting against the hand of God." She went on to discuss the Supreme Court Justice positions that were empty. So instead of talking about the goodness of Jesus or how important salvation is or how the body of Christ needs to pray more to bring not

just this country together but also bring the church back together, this election not only caused further division within the country but it also caused a major divide within the church. She spent most of her time on the network speaking to millions of people lifting up man instead of lifting up the name of Jesus. I consider that to be a missed opportunity to talk to millions of people about the glory of God instead of the Glory of man. I really believe as Christians, our focus can be misguided at times, and sometimes, we need to go back to the basics of focusing more on God and his Truth instead of our truth.

After listening to this prominent pastor's commentary, I really had to pray and put aside my own feelings in order to really understand what was happening in that moment. I was dealing with so many mixed emotions regarding the aftermath of the election. So, I really had to go to the Word to try and understand where she was coming from. And the Word does say that God is the one that ultimately gives the authority of position. "Let every person be subject to the governing authorities. For there is no authority except from God (granted by His permission and sanction), and those which exist have been put in place by God (granted by His permission and sanction). Therefore, whoever resists (governmental) authority resists the ordinance of God. And those who have resisted it will bring judgment (civil penalty) on themselves." *Romans13:1-2*

So I do believe God allowed the outcome of this election in the same way he allowed Judas Iscariot, one of the twelve apostles, to betray Jesus for thirty pieces of silver by conspiring with the chief priest and the elders to plot and plan to have Jesus arrested, which in turn led to a path of pain and suffering for Jesus. A suffering that could not and cannot compare to any other suffering in this world—he was beaten and bruised for our iniquities. That in itself helped me to look at the bigger picture of his crucifixion, which I know, accomplished the eternal redemption of man. So, yes, in this situation, God allowed one of his own (Judas Iscariot) to be used by Satan to start the process of Salvation. "Then one of the twelve, who was called Judas Iscariot, went to the chief priest and said, 'what are you willing to give me if I hand Jesus over to you?' And they weighed out thirty pieces of silver. And from that moment, Judas began looking for an opportune time to betray Jesus." *Matthew 26:14-16*

God also allowed the devil to test Job. "Then Satan answered the Lord, 'Does Job fear God for nothing? Have you not put a hedge of protection around him and his house, and all that he has on every side? You have blessed the work of his hands, and conferred prosperity and happiness upon him, and his possessions have increased in the land. But put forth your hand now and touch (destroy) all that he has, and he will surely curse you to your face'. Then the Lord said to Satan, 'Behold, all that Job has is in your power, only do not put your hand on the man himself'. So Satan was allowed to take everything except Job's life. But Job did not turn his back on God, nor did he curse God. After Job went through the trials and distress and the pain of losing his entire family, he continued to honor God. After Job endured the test, God restored him and his latter was greater than his former. So the Lord blessed the latter end of Job more than his beginning: for he had fourteen thousand sheep, and six thousand camels, and a thousand yoke of oxen, and one thousand female donkeys." *Job 42:12*

I know after reading Job some people had the same question I did: why did God allow Satan to test Job in such a manner? Well, only God himself can answer that question but we do know from the Scriptures, why God puts us through the fire of trials and tribulations. I came across a wonderful article on Bible Way Mag, The Christian magazine of choice, titled, '6 Reasons The Lord Test You And Put You Through Trials' written by Eston Swaby, and it gave some pointers on why God sometimes puts us through trials. According to the article, Point One was to refine us. 'Refine' is, 'to bring to a fine or a pure state, free from impurities: to refine metal, sugar, or petroleum'; 'to purify from what is coarse, vulgar, or debasing; make elegant or cultured'; 'to bring to a finer state or form by purifying'; 'to make more fine, subtle, or precise'. He based his first premise on *Zachariah 13:9*: "And I will bring the third part through the fire, refine them as silver is refined, and test them as gold is tested. They will call on my name, and I will listen and answer them; I will say, they are my people, And they will say, 'The Lord is my God'. God was refining his children. Like anything else that needs to be refined, there is a process that has to take place in our lives, and at times, it can be grueling. Sometimes it feels like the process will never end. We have to hold on to the fact that everything has a time to end and once it is finished, we will come out like pure gold. The greater the assignment, the greater the test will be. God has to make sure we are up for the task. Our trials are used to build up our faith and him, so we can get to a level of non-wavering trust in him, no matter what comes our way.

Point Two was, "to prove to Satan and the world that we are children of God". He based the premise on *1 Peter 1:7.* I would include verses (3-7): "Blessed be the God and Father of our Lord Jesus Christ, who according to His abundant and boundless mercy, has caused us to be born again (that is, to be reborn from above—spiritually transformed, renewed, and set apart for His purpose) to an ever-living hope and confident assurance through the resurrection of Jesus Christ from the dead,(born anew) into an inheritance which is imperishable (beyond the reach of change) and defiled and unfading, reserved in heaven for you, who are being protected and shielded by the power of God through your faith for salvation that is ready to be revealed(for you) in the last time. In this you rejoice greatly, even though now for a little while, if necessary, you have been distressed by various trials, so that the genuineness of your faith, which is much more precious than gold which is perishable, even though tested and purified by fire, may be found to result in (your) praise and glory and honor at the revelation of Jesus Christ." In one of his letters to the saints that where suffering persecution, he wrote to them to tell that the trials and testing they are undergoing was to prove to the world that they are genuine Christians, yes, real not phony. "And to also see what they are made of. By their endurance people will come to know and may even serve the God they serve, that the trials and testing they are undergoing is to prove to the world that they are genuine Christians."

Point Three was, "God may want to bless you." *Job 1:6-22:* "Many times we are going through some thing because God wants to bless us, but to do that, we must go through some trials. We must be tested. The trials you go through are not to destroy you, but they are to elevate you. It may not be that the Lord wants to bless you materially, but he may want to promote you at your job, in the ministry or any form of exaltation. When you endure the hardship, then you will fully understand what the Lord was doing and you will have joy."

Point Four, "God will test you and put you through trials so that you may know him more." *Job 42:5:* "I had heard of you (only) by the hearing of the ear, but now my (spiritual) eye sees you." Like with Job, as Christians, we started our relationship with God based upon what we heard and learned about him but once we start going through all sorts of trials and begin to have firsthand knowledge of how awesome he is by the trials and tribulations we go through; this helps us to draw near to him and get to know the nature of God. When we start to spend more time with him, that's when the relationship begins to develop.

Point Five was, "To help you grow." He touched on the fact that we can learn from prior bad experiences and we can somehow mature from trials, if we don't allow our experiences to break us and make us bitter. I believe sometimes God wants to know that we love him above all else. As Christians, we have to come to terms and accept that in this life, testing is a part of our journey and we cannot fear or run from the process if we want to pass the test and move to the next level in God. *1 Peter 5:10*: "After you have suffered for a little while, the God of all grace (who imparts His blessing and favor), who called you to His own eternal glory in Christ, will Himself complete, confirm, strengthen, and establish you (making you what you ought to be). He wants to see if we will still stand and trust him in the face of adversity. Point Six: "How will I know when the Lord is testing me?" According to the author, God will not always let us know when he is testing us but he will give us the strength to endure and pass the test. He referenced *1 Corinthians 10:13:* "No temptation (regardless of its source) has overtaken or enticed you that is not common to human experience (nor is any temptation unusual or beyond human resistance); but God is faithful (to His word-He is compassionate and trustworthy), and He will not let you be tempted beyond your ability (to resist), but along with the temptation He (has in the past and is now and) will (always) provide the way out as well, so that you will be able to endure it (without yielding, and will overcome temptation with joy)." So no matter what the challenge, he will equip us to handle anything that comes our way if we would just trust him.

I would like to give you another example of God allowing an event or circumstance to take place to help further his plan. One name that comes to mind is Joseph. God allowed Joseph's brothers to sell him into slavery in Egypt. They were pawns in his plans to set Joseph up for greatness and eventually save a nation from starvation. "And it came to pass, when Joseph was come unto his brethren, that they stripped Joseph out of his coat, his coat of many colors that was on him; and they took him, and cast him into a pit: and the pit was empty, there was no water in it. And they sat down to eat bread: and they lifted up their eyes and looked, and, behold, a company of Ishmaelites came from Gilead, with their camels bearing spicery and balm and myrrh, going to carry it down to Egypt. And Judah said unto his brethren, what profit is it if we slay our brother, and conceal his blood? Come, and let us sell him to the Ishmaelites, and let not our hand be upon him; for he is our brother and our flesh; and his brethren were content. Then there passed by Mid'i-anites merchantmen; and they drew and lifted up Joseph out of the pit, and sold Joseph to the Ishmaelites for twenty pieces of silver: and they brought Joseph into Egypt." *Genesis 37:23-28* Because of jealousy and evil, Joseph was sold into slavery but because he was a part of God's master plan, he was put into a position of wealth and power to carry out the supreme plan of God. "But Joseph said to them, 'Do not be afraid, for you, you meant evil against me, but God meant it for good in order to bring about this present outcome, that many people would be kept alive (as they are this day). So now, do not be afraid; I will provide for you and support you and your little ones'. So he comforted them, giving them encouragement and hope, and spoke (with kindness) to their hearts." *Genesis 50:19-21*

He has a strategy in everything that he does. There are many examples in the Bible of controversial evil leaders that God allowed to rise to power for his purpose and plan. Let's take a look at Herod Antipater, known by the nickname of Antipas, who was a 1st century ruler of Galilee and Perea, also known as King Herod. Antipas was a weak man, who ordered the death of John the Baptist. *Mark 6:27-28* "So the King immediately sent for an executioner and commanded him to bring back John's head. And he went and had John beheaded in the prison, and brought back his head on a platter, and gave it to the girl; and the girl gave it to her mother." Antipas also stood in judgment of Jesus Christ when Pontius Pilate felt incapable of the task. "Antipas, expecting a miracle, was annoyed at Jesus' silence, so he sent him back to Pilate to be murdered upon the demands of the Jews." I guess you can say that he did not have the best character and leadership skills, so why did God allow Antipas to be put in a position of authority that ultimately led to the death of his only son? It was all a part of God's master plan. Antipas was just another pawn used to get Jesus to the right place, which was back in front of Pilate to be sentence to his death on the cross. This allowed the accomplishment of His supreme goal—the death and Resurrection of Jesus Christ. The Resurrection led to our salvation, so yes, thank God for Antipas and Pilot being in a position of authority at the right time and for the right reason.

I believe, as Christians, we have to retrain our minds to make God the focal point of our lives. Once we begin to lose focus, we have to go back to the basics, and that consists of prayer and staying in the presence of God. His presence allows us to gain access to his kingdom and remove the clutter of the world that consumes our minds every day. This will help us to refocus. So, the words spoken by the prominent pastor I mentioned earlier had some foundational points, such as we have to pray for our leaders and lift them up to God, so that they can get the direction they need to make the important decisions for the well-being of the country. But do we just dismiss all the turmoil and wickedness that the King is inflicting upon the people? We have to pray for every President during their time in office, regardless of whether we agree with their policies or not. The word of God is the word of God; it never changes, and we cannot alter it to fit our political views. I may be wrong but I do not recall any pastors in the past lifting any other President in history up to be a King that God put into office, nor do I recall this particular pastor or any other pastor rebuking their critics. Please believe me when I say I mean no disrespect but as Christians, when we are applying the Word to justify an action or reaction, we have to make sure we do not create a double standard.

In first *Samuel 8:4-21,* the children of Israel begged God for a king, and even though they were warned of the risk and the consequences they would suffer from the king, they chose to ignore the warning so

God gave them what they asked for, and because they did not trust God to lead them, they had to endure hardship due to that evil King. "Then all elders of Israel gathered together and came to Samuel at Ramah and said to him, 'Look, you have grown old, and your sons do not walk in your ways. Now appoint us a king to judge us (and rule over us) like all the other nations'. But their demand displeased Samuel when they said, "Give us a king to judge and rule over us." So, Samuel prayed to the Lord. The Lord said to Samuel, "Listen to the voice of the people in regard to all that they say to you, for they have not rejected you, but they have rejected me from being king over them. Like all the deeds which they have done since the day that I brought them up from Egypt even to this day—in that they have abandoned (rejected) Me and served other gods—so they are doing to you also. So now listen to their voice; only solemnly warn them and tell them the ways of the king who will reign over them." So Samuel told all the words of the Lord to the people who were asking him for a king. He said, "These will be the ways of the king who will reign over you: he will take your sons and appoint them for himself to his chariots and among his horsemen, and they will run before his chariots. He will appoint them for himself to be commanders over thousands and over fifties, and some to do his plowing and to reap his harvest and to make his implements of war and equipment for his chariots. He will take your daughters to be perfumers, cooks, and bakers. He will take the best of your fields, your vineyards, and your olive groves, and give them to his servants. He will take a tenth of your grain and of your vineyards and give it to his officers and to his servants. He will take your male servants and your best young men and your donkeys and use them for his work. He will take a tenth of your flocks, and you yourselves shall be his servants. Then you will cry out on that day because of your king whom you have chosen for yourselves, but the Lord will not answer you on that day (because you have rejected Him as King)." Nevertheless, the people refused to listen to the voice of Samuel, and they said, "No, but there shall be a king over us, so that we too may be like all the nations (around us), that our king may judge (and govern) us and go out before us and fight our battles." Samuel had heard all the words of the people and repeated them to the Lord. And the Lord said to Samuel, "Listen to their request and appoint a king for them." So Samuel said to the men of Israel, "Go, each man to his own city."

We have all heard the saying, 'Be careful what you wish for, lest it come true' and 'be careful what you wish for; you may receive it.' According to Idiom definition this means, "If you get things that you desire, there may be unforeseen and unpleasant consequences. I can understand the individuals that feel they were not being heard by the leaders in Washington and they wanted a drastic change and they believed the promises of the current leadership. We know that ignorance and hate is what motivated the extremist, racist, and white nationalists to further their cause. But what I am still having a hard time understanding is how eighty percent of our fellow Evangelicals voted for this result, even after seeing and hearing what the entire world witnessed. I am also a believer and I know we have our own experiences and opinions but we have one common goal as Christians— the Gospel of Jesus Christ. The gospel should reflect upon every area of our lives. So, if this is who God chose to lead this country, as some people have said, it may be a part of a much bigger plan; or could it simply be the fact that the people had a choice to make, and they made it. Please don't get me wrong. I believe God is sovereign and he can assert his authority in any circumstance if he chooses to do so. The key phrase is—if he chooses to do so. He encourages us to do the right thing and make the right choices but since the beginning, he has given us free will, and that comes with choices and consequences. The choice to accept the call… the choice to love and receive him as our savior… the choice to have a relationship with him… The Word says in *Galatians: 5:13*, "You, my brothers and sisters, were called to be free. But do not use your freedom to indulge the flesh; rather, serve one another humbly in love." "Anyone who chooses to do the will of God will find out whether my teaching comes from God or whether I speak on my own." *John 7:17*

The choices we make can also impact our destiny either positively or negatively. Even though God gives us free will, we have to make a conscious decision to align our will with his by getting to know him on a personal level, staying in his presence and reading his word, and definitely by allowing his spirit to lead us and guide us. "The earth is the domain of decisions. It is where human beings have the right to choose good or evil, blessings or curses, success or failure, life-or-death." (*The Art of War for Spiritual Battle*, Cindy Trimm)

We should never second-guess what we know to be right or wrong. I have heard some Christians say that God is in control of every circumstance, and he would have not allowed the result of this election, if it wasn't in his will. A year after the election, I still find myself struggling with the result being that the country is more divided than ever before. I still wonder if this was his will for us. If we go back to *1st Samuel 8:4-22*, was it the will of God for the children of Israel to have a king? God told Samuel to let them know they did not need a king, and to just trust him but they had to have a King, and because they did not trust God, they suffered the consequences.

So, whether we believe the result of the 2016 election lined up with the will of God or not, nothing can disrupt or alter his plan. God knows the end from the beginning. So, no, the 2016 election did not catch God off-guard, nor did it shock him because once again he always has a master plan. It gives me great comfort to know that no matter what, we win. We know the Word of God says in *Isaiah 46:10*, "Declaring the end and the result from the beginning, And from ancient times the things which have not (yet) been done, Saying, 'My purpose will be established, And I will do all that pleases me and fulfills my purpose." As Christians, sometimes we make decisions that do not always line up with the will of God for our lives but his grace and his mercy are sufficient and are renewed daily."And from his fullness, we have all received grace upon grace." *John 1:16*

"For the grace of God has appeared, bringing salvation for all people, training us to renounce ungodliness and worldly passions, and to live self-controlled, upright, and godly lives in the present age, waiting for our blessed hope, the appearing of the glory of our great God and Savior Jesus Christ, who gave himself for us, to redeem us from all lawlessness and to purify for himself a people for his own possession, who are zealous for good works." *Titus 2:11-14*

"It is of the Lord's mercies that we are not consumed, because his compassions fail not. They are new every morning: great is thy faithfulness." *Lamentations 3:22-23 King James Version.*

Is it possible the election of the first African-American President was the catalyst that determined the results of the 2016 election? Is it possible God allowed the rise of President Donald Trump to unmask the deep-rooted racism that still exists in and outside of the church? Could it be that he is simple trying to get us to see through our spiritual eyes what is so clear concerning his church? I believe God is going to use the choice of his people regarding the 2016 election to serve a greater purpose, and that purpose is connected to a greater plan to reveal, revive, unite and redirect his church back to what is important—winning souls for the kingdom of God. If we were honest about what is going on in this country, we would reexamine our hearts and values to decide if our Christian values are lining up with the Word of God. I do not know of any part of his Word that teaches us to support or ignore anyone who supports or indulges in any form of hate, racism, violence and or discrimination. When making impactful life-changing decisions, it is important that we pray for direction. After the election, I had to seek God more and more; whenever we seek the face of God, he gives us clarity and peace. Even in our darkest times, he can shine on us and provide his light in the darkness.

I know some of you are still feeling a sense of hopelessness, and yes, even maybe betrayal. But if we can just tap into that peace that surpasses all understanding, keeping our eyes on him, we can have peace in the storm. We have to continue to pray for each other and try to understand one another. We must deal with each other in love, without fear or hate—even when we disagree with each other. We can make it through anything together as one body in Christ but for us to get to that point, we have to first get to the truth of what divides us. It is not always an easy task to seek for and receive the truth but it is a necessity for all believers because it is the core of who we are in Christ Jesus.

CHAPTER 2

What is happening to the church?

I just recently read an interesting article written by Daniel Burke, CNN Religion Editor. It mentioned that a study found that millennials are leaving the church in droves. The article was written in May of 2015. The highlight of the story was a survey conducted by Pew Research Center, which showed Christian population dropping to 70%—it found that more than one-third of millennials said they were unaffiliated with any faith. The survey of 35,000 American adults showed the Christian percentage of the population dropping. The study also found that almost every major branch of Christianity in the United States had lost a significant number of members, mainly because millennials were leaving the fold. This demographic group saw a significant drop in people who call themselves Christians—more than one-third of millennials said they were unaffiliated with any faith—up 10 percentage points since 2007, according to the article. It also stated that according to the study done by Pew, "It's not just millennials leaving the church. Whether married or single, rich or poor, young or old, living in the West or the Bible belt, almost every demographic group has seen a significant drop in people who call themselves Christians." Greg Smith, Pew's associate director of religion research, said, "We've known that the (number of) religiously unaffiliated has been growing for decades. But the pace at which they've continued to grow is really astounding." When I read those statistics, it didn't surprise me because you can see it every Sunday in most churches across the nation. And if you ask most leaders, they could probably give you more insight into the falling numbers of people attending church on a regular basis. I have young adult children. When I gave my twenty-six-year-old son those statistics, he wasn't in the least bit surprised. He told me that a great deal of the younger generation views the church as judgmental and oftentimes hypocritical; sometimes they have a difficult time relating to the church. As Christians, we have to focus on the next generation and how to win them back. We have to make sure that we stay in tune with the will of God when it comes to reaching our young people. It is so crucial for leaders to have a close relationship with Jesus Christ in order to see the true gift within the people that God has entrusted them with.

I would like to share a true story about two siblings that were young and impressionable, and started off using their gifts in the church. They both were gifted with the ability to sing and write music, and they had been singing and dancing since they were two and three years of age. Even though the siblings were seven years apart in age, and were gifted in different areas of music, they both shared the same love of music. The sister could sing, write music, and create melodies. The brother could sing, and with his worship, usher in the presence of God into a room. He had the potential to be a great worship leader one day. The two siblings decided to join the Praise and Worship Team at the church they attended. The Praise and Worship Team was full of young adults. The siblings were flourishing in the team, and enjoying going to every service singing to the glory of God. They had formed a bond with the team. The atmosphere in the sanctuary was saturated with the presence of God during every service.

One day the worship leader announced that he was leaving, and that was the start of a downward spiral. The pastor hired a temporary worship leader who was well-known and very talented. But Sunday after Sunday, the atmosphere during service changed, and some members of the Worship Team began to leave the ministry. The siblings, however, remained faithful even though they did not feel the same bond and joy they felt in the past. Serving became more of a task than joy, so eventually, the sister went away to school, and the brother remained faithful. Finally one Sunday, when the part-time worship leader was away at another event, the remaining sibling got his opportunity to lead a worship song. His worship during that service changed the atmosphere to what it once was before the sudden change. You could sense the anointing of the oil all over that young man, so much so that the members of the congregation came up to the young man after the service to let him know how much they enjoyed his worship. So you can imagine how confused and discouraged the young man became when service went back to the status quo that next Sunday. The young man hung in there for a month, until finally, his spirit was broken. After a month or so, he too quit out of frustration. One Sunday, he was sitting down with the congregation during the worship service, and next thing you know, he was no longer a part of the ministry that his gift was meant for. The saddest fact about this story is that instead of someone from the leadership reaching out to the young man, the leadership eventually tried to push him into the media ministry, which included recording the services, and taking pictures and posting them on social media. This, in turn, pushed the siblings away from the ministry altogether. I am not sure if the leadership just did not recognize the gift in the siblings, or maybe the need to have the media position filled became a larger priority. The result is almost three years later the body of Christ has two young adults not using their gifts for the kingdom of God. It is important for leaders to stay close to the source to develop sensitivity towards them, to remain vigilant, and to assist in developing the gifts within the sheep. After all, souls are more important than positions.

1 Peter 4:10 "Just as each one of you has received a special gift (a spiritual talent, an ability graciously given by God), employ it in serving one another as (is appropriate for) good stewards of God's multi-faceted grace (faithfully using the diverse, varied gifts and abilities granted to Christians by God's unmerited favor)." We must continue to seek God for direction on how to change the negative view of the church. As believers, we have to be mindful of our actions; realizing we are ambassadors for Christ, so our words do matter. We should be consistently praying that God will direct us on how to reach the next generation. I believe that it is critical that as believers, we are in tune with all the challenges that millennials are facing. We have to use effective communication to reach out to the next generation, and that does not always mean we should be speaking. Sometimes, it's better to just listen; sometimes, we can learn and accomplish more by just staying silent. As Christians, we want to understand everything but we often forget that God's ways are higher than our ways, his thoughts are higher than our thoughts. We have to ask the Holy Spirit to help us see people as God sees them. We have to love people with the love of God, and that means with flaws and all, no matter what a person's skin color is, what their beliefs are, and no matter what lifestyle they choose to live.

I know we can accomplish this as Christians, if we stay close to God's love. We have to remember that our supreme purpose as

Christians is to aid in winning souls for the kingdom of God through the Holy Spirit guiding us and by our God-given assignments. We should be walking in our purpose daily but often; it is hard to do. We have so many distractions in our lives that it becomes difficult to focus on what is important—purpose. Most of us develop so many wounds throughout our lifetime that we hold onto, and this in turn stops us from being whole. We have to recognize that as long as we live on this earth, there will always be problems that we will come up against. But the wonderful thing is, if we have a relationship with Jesus Christ—the one who died for our sins and rose again—we will come out on the winning side. We will never face those problems alone if we stay close to the source and never let go. The tighter the grip, the better-off we will be. "My soul clings to you; your right hand upholds me." *Psalm 63:8*

As Christians, we often fail to realize how important it is that we stay under the wings and protection of God by praying and staying in constant communion with him, especially in the volatile times that we are living in. We can know him by praying and staying in constant communion with him, which will help us in forming a relationship. The more we get to know him, the more we will know and become who we were called to be in Christ Jesus, and this will bring us closer to walking in our purpose. The church is supposed to be a refuge for the lost and the brokenhearted. It's more than just any old building. It should be a place for us to feel safe and secure, a place of forgiveness and love without strife... A place where as soon as you walk into the doors, you feel the love and peace of Christ. So, if this is the case, why do we have people leaving the church in droves? The foundation of the church is important to the structure of the church. If the foundation is not solid, then the structure will begin to crumble all around the foundation.

I recently went to a training session dealing with promoting church growth. An interesting thing that I learned was that most of the church models today are modeled after a corporation or a democracy. The democracy consists of members, who could be compared to registered voters. In an election, they have a vote and they use that vote to determine who the President and the members of Congress will be. In this church model, the members get to vote for a pastor and decide how long that pastor will get to lead. They also have the power to select a board and vote the board members and the pastor out. In the corporate model, you have a CEO who is in charge of the company along with a board of directors, shareholders who own shares, and they are considered voting members of the corporation. How is a church compared to a corporation? In my research, I found that in this model, the pastor is the CEO; the Deacon Board is compared to the board of directors in a corporation; the congregation represents the stockholders, who have their annual meeting to vote on how the business should operate. The pastor and board of directors head the church, and just as in a Fortune 500 company, the stockholders can vote the board members and the CEO out of office. So, should the church mirror a corporation or a democracy? Or maybe the answer is neither.

When doing my research on the different models of the structure of the church, I came across a lesson from Bible.org entitled 'Who's in charge of the church?' It talked about the fact that most American Christians, if asked, would say, the pastor is in charge of the church. The lesson also emphasized how many American pastors are burning out, and are quitting because they are so overwhelmed by the responsibilities of running the church. It also talked about most of them feeling exhausted and getting nowhere. "As a church grows, the pastor's role often changes imperceptibly into a business manager rather than a pastor-teacher." To prevent these problems, we need to answer from the Bible, who is in charge of the church? The lesson took me to *(Eph.1:20-23)*, "which he produced in Christ when He raised Him from the dead and seated Him at His own right hand in the heavenly places, far above all rule and authority and power and dominion (whether angelic or human), and (far above) every name that is named (above every title that can be conferred), not only in this age and world but also in the one to come. And He put all things (in every realm) in subjection under Christ's feet, and appointed Him as (supreme and authoritative) head over all things in the church, which is His body, the fullness of Him who fills and completes all things in all believers." So that just says it all when answering the question of who's in charge of the church. It is very simple and straightforward—Jesus is in charge of his church. I will take it even further and ask the question, do we, as believers, treat him as the head? Or are we so caught up in pleasing man that we forget the basic principles that help keep us in the right order with God. The Church is neither a democratic organization nor is it a corporation, therefore it should not be treated as such. I thought it was deep when the author of this lesson stated, "The key question in church government is not, what is the mind of the members? But, what is the mind of Christ?

The Church is a living organism, with Jesus Christ as the living head." Organism, according to Merriam-Webster's Dictionary, is, "a form of life composed of mutually interdependent parts that maintain various vital processes." The definition of organization according to Webster is," an administrative and functional structure." As a body of believers, we are the Church and although we may work independently, we need each other to survive. When you think about parts of the body, each organ is important and has a unique job, so the body can work to its full capacity. The brain, heart and the lungs are the most important organs in the body —each organ is significant on its own but the organs also need each other to survive. Without the three parts, the whole body will die. The brain is responsible for transmitting messages to the rest of the body and for our senses and perception, thoughts, motivation, arousal, learning, movement and general functioning. It is also responsible for the way we process information. The heart handles circulating blood, nutrients and oxygen to the rest of the body and without the circulation of blood, it would be impossible for us to live. The lungs are important to our respiratory system —the lungs control the body's breathing. The principal role of the lungs is to exchange oxygen, which is inhaled with carbon dioxide found in the blood. The heart is the centerpiece between the brain and the lungs; death will come without the centerpiece pumping the blood to reach the brain and the lungs. In the same way, the human body is unable to sustain life without the brain, heart and lungs, as Christians, we will die spiritually, if we do not have a sound connection to the Trinity. Trinity, according to dictionary.com, is "Also called Blessed Trinity, Holy Trinity, the union of three persons (Father, Son, and Holy Ghost) in one Godhead, or the threefold personality of the Divine Being." "Go ye therefore, and teach all nations, baptizing them in the name of the Father, and of the Son, and of the Holy Ghost." *Matthew 28:19*

"For there are three that bear record in heaven, the Father, the Word, and the Holy Ghost: and these three are one." *1 John 5:7-8* "The Word represents Jesus Christ in the flesh. And the Word was made flesh, and dwelt among us, (and we beheld his glory, the glory as of the only begotten of the Father,) full of grace and truth. *John 1:14.*

As Christians, it is important for us to stay connected to the source; in the same way that the connection between the brain, heart and lungs is vital to the human body, the Father, Son (the Word) and the Holy Spirit are just as vital to the Body of Christ, (the Church), to survive. Are we totally connected to the center of the Trinity, which would be Jesus Christ, of course, because it was the shedding of his blood that connects us to the other parts of the Trinity? As Christians, we need each part to survive, and you cannot have one without the other because they are one.

I will ask the question again, what has happened to the Church? Could it be that the church is shrinking? According to the dictionary, the definition of shrinking is "to draw back, as in retreat or avoidance: to shrink from danger; to shrink from contact, to contract or reduce in size, as from exposure to conditions." Is it possible the conditions that are causing the church to shrink are related to disobedience and sin? You may be wondering: how is the church being disobedient? The Word of God gives us instructions on how to live a life that is, for one, pleasing to him, two, helping us in fulfilling our purpose in him. But sometimes, we override or just ignore those instructions. For instance, the Word teaches us to pray without ceasing, so we can stay connected to him. This will assist us in forming a relationship with Jesus Christ. "Pray continually." *1 Thessalonians 5:17* What does it mean to pray without ceasing? To "pray without ceasing" refers to being consistent in prayer, recurring prayer. Prayer should be, for all Christians, a way of life. But I would ask, how many Christians can honestly say that they follow this command? "If my people, who are called by my name, will humble themselves and pray and seek my face and turn from their wicked ways, then I will hear from heaven, and I will forgive their sin and will heal their land." *2 Chronicles 7:14*

I will ask again, are we, as Christians, following that command? I would say, not wholeheartedly. For instance, when the leader of a church calls for corporate prayer, you can usually count the amount of people that show up for prayer on your fingers. Is this considered disobedience? The Word of God teaches us not to judge. "Judge not, that you be not judged." *Matthew 7:1* As Christians, sometimes we are often judgmental but we all have something about ourselves that we need to work on. "For everyone has sinned; and fall short of the glory of God."

Romans 3:23 Wow! No one is perfect. As Christians, we will all make mistakes but the important thing is that when we do make a mistake, we acknowledge the mistake, repent and forgive ourselves and move forward. I want you to marinate on all the questions asked in this chapter, and as you begin to receive revelation, I believe the truth will set you free and richly bless you!

CHAPTER 3

The sleeping giant!

Is the church asleep? 'Asleep' according to Dictionary.com means 'in or into a state of sleep: into a dormant or inactive state; to rest.' I ask if the Church could be asleep because of a dream that I had maybe around two years ago. In the dream, my kids and I were at a church service and the pastor had just finished preaching. I could see me and my kids sleeping but the most disturbing part of the dream was that the members and the leaders of the church did not recognize that we were asleep. When the service was over, everyone left us sleeping in the church. When we awoke from our slumber, the church was dark and the doors were locked. Many months after the dream, I was in prayer one morning. I had a flashback of that particular dream, and I could hear the words within my spirit— 'sleeping giant'! It wasn't hard to put it all together, the dream and the phrase, 'the sleeping giant'! Could it be that the church is 'the sleeping giant'? Has the church forgotten the power it possesses? I am not speaking of the power received through status or political means but I mean the power that is received through the Trinity. The power that we can obtain when we receive the keys to the kingdom., "I will give you the keys (authority) of the kingdom of heaven; and whatever you bind (forbid, declare to be improper and unlawful) on earth will have already been bound in heaven, and whatever you loose (permit, declare lawful) on earth will have (already) been loosed in heaven." *Matthew 16:19 NIV.* "They will act religious, but they will reject the power that could make them godly. Stay away from people like that!" *2 Timothy 3:5*

Being morally right and religious is not the same as having a true relationship with Jesus Christ; according to Dictionary.com, religion is, 'a set of beliefs concerning the cause, nature, and purpose of the universe, especially when considered as the creation of a superhuman agency or agencies, usually involving devotional and ritual observances, and often containing a moral code governing the conduct of human affairs; the practice of religious beliefs, ritual observance of faith.' Could it be that the church is so stuck in tradition and rituals that it may be missing the true move of God, derailing the believer from receiving the genuine essence of God? 'Derail' means 'to cause to fail or become deflected from a purpose; reduce or delay the chances for success or development.' Could it be that rituals, traditions and programs are interfering with the body staying connected to the source? Churches have to spend more time on the word of God— the most important part of the service—and less time on programs and reading the announcements for the week. Maybe the word of God should be delivered during the middle of the service directly after the worship service, keeping the flow of the anointing moving directly into the word—making it that much effective. I mean that's just food for thought.

I recently read another very interesting article called, '13 signs of a dying church written by, Joseph Mattera, "The Word of God teaches us that there are times God's presence can leave the corporate expression of His people. We see this in *1 Samuel 4:21-22* when the name Ichabod was given to the grandson of Eli, the high priest, after the ark of the covenant was captured by the Philistines." According to Wikipedia, 'Ichabod' means, "no glory, inglorious or where is the glory? 1 Samuel 4:21-22 says, "And she named the boy Ichabod, saying, "The glory has left Israel," because the ark of God had been taken and because of the deaths of her father-in-law and her husband. 22 She said, "The glory has left Israel, for the ark of God has been taken." The article also talked about, "In the Book of *Revelation 3:1*, Jesus told the church of Sardis that it had a reputation of being alive but was dead. Hence, it is possible for communities of faith to be dead or dying." I will dive a little deeper and look at Revelation 3:2-3 "Wake up, and strengthen and reaffirm what remains of your faithful commitment to Me, which is about to die; for I have not found any of your deeds completed in the sight of My God or meeting His requirements. 3 So remember and take to heart the lessons you have received and heard. Keep and obey them, and repent change your sinful way of thinking, and demonstrate your repentance with new behavior that proves a conscious decision to turn away from sin. So then, if you do not wake up, I will come like a thief, and you will not know at what hour I will come to you." The article also referenced *Revelation 2:4-5,* "But I have this charge against you that you have left your first love (you have lost the depth of love that you first had for me)." 5. "So remember the heights from which you have fallen, and repent (change your inner self, your old way of thinking, your sinful behavior seek God's will) and do the works you did at first (when you first knew me); otherwise, I will visit you and remove your lamp stand (the church, its impact) from its place unless you repent." It's high time that church wakes up and take its rightful place. The article went on to say, "Since the lamp stand represents the church, according to *Revelation 1:20,* then Jesus was either threatening to shut down the church and or remove Himself from it- which would mean it was dead spiritually. Since Jesus said that the gates of hell cannot prevail against the church (Matt. 16), then it is impossible for Satan to close down a church; whenever a church ceases to exist, it is the Lord Himself who shut it down." Mr. Mattera believes this is the reason why in the next few decades many denominations will cease to exist as well as why many congregations will be closing their doors every year.

The article listed 13 signs of a dead or dying church that I thought was interesting. Number one being, "There are no functional prayer gatherings. Within dying churches, few people show up to pray and seek God together since they have no sense of His presence or that He is present in the midst of them, just as you would not be motivated to speak to your friend if you didn't think they were listening. Number two was, 'There is no expectation of answered prayers.' Few if any pray together since there is no anticipation that God will actually answer prayer. When you are in a church without faith to believe God, it is either dead or dying. Number three, 'The presence of God is missing in the assembly of the saints.' Metaphorically, the heavens are like brass over the skies of dead or dying churches. (Deut. 28:23). There is no sense of God's presence during worship even though Jesus promised that where two or three gatherers in His name, He is in the midst of them. (Matt.*18:20)* Number four, 'The power of God is not manifest.' Jesus said that when demons were cast out it was a sign the kingdom of God was among them (Luke *11:20)* The apostle Paul expected the miraculous to be the norm in the life of the church, as we read in *Galatians 3:5. "* "So then, does He who supplies you with His Spirit and works miracles among you, do it as a result of the works of the Law (which you perform), or because you (believe confidently in the message which you) heard with faith?" The article touched on that Jesus expects us to trust him and use our faith to believe that we will receive the answers to our prayers. We have to expect results when we pray according to the will of God. When there is no sign of the manifested presence of God, or of 'God's divine intervention in a church, it can be a sign the church is dead or dying.' Number five was, "The Word of God is presented without authority or anointing." This to me signals, the leader that is preaching the word using the authority on the inside pulling from the spirit of God instead of their flesh. The article referenced (Mark. 1:22). "They were completely amazed at His teaching; because He was teaching them as one having (God-given) authority, and not as the scribes." Number six, Few, if any, people are saved or get baptized. When there are no people being saved or baptized, it is a sign the Lord is no longer working in their midst. (*Acts 2:47) says,* "Praising God continually, and having favor with all the people. And the Lord kept adding to the church daily those who were being saved." What does it mean when fewer and fewer people are giving their lives to Christ and joining the church? Number seven, "Every church service is predictable by the minute." No matter the type of church, if every aspect of the service is predictable from the time you enter the doors up until the time the service has ended, the worship, the preaching, taking up the offering, the announcements, are all choreographed to the minute, then according to the article, "it may reveal there is no room for the Holy Spirit to operate. Like Samson of old, the Spirit may have departed without the people knowing it (Judges 16:20). "She said, "The Philistines are upon you, Samson!" And he awoke from sleep and said, "I will go out as I have time after time and shake myself free. "For Samson did not know that the Lord had departed from him." Truly, any aspect of our church that can function without dependence on the Holy Spirit shows that it is a machination of men and not God. Number eight, 'There is no pattern of disciple making.' Mr. Mattera explained, "The bottom line in all churches is the making of committed Christ followers, better known as disciples. It doesn't matter how large a church is, what matters is how many mature sons are being developed that will positively affect the created order." He referenced (Rom. 8:19-21). Where is that drive to win souls and developed more disciples for the Kingdom of God. Number nine, The people jockey for position and titles. According to Mr. Mattera, "When people are not seeking the glory of God, they depend even more upon getting affirmation from men. Hence, a church without the presence of God will most likely have a hierarchical culture with people posturing for positions and titles. The less you know God intimately, the more your identity will be connected to credentials and titles." Number ten, 'There is no divine sense of mission and purpose.' "When there is no vision, the people are perishing; when a congregation is dead or dying, they have no compelling transcendent purpose that motivates them to fulfill their biblical calling. (*Proverbs 29:18*)

"Where there is no vision, (no revelation of God and His word), the people are unrestrained;

"But happy and blessed is he who keeps the law (of God)." Number eleven, 'Few people volunteer to serve.' *Psalm 110:3* "Your people will offer themselves willingly (to participate in your battle) in the day of your power; in the splendor of holiness, from the womb of the dew." "Consequently, in dead or dying churches very few people volunteer to serve in the ministry." Number twelve, 'Few people support the church with tithes and offerings.' Jesus said, in *Matt. 6:21* "For where your treasure is, there your heart (your wishes, your desires; that on which your life centers) will be also." So basically, if people feel the church is not moving in the right direction, fewer people will be willing or motivated to continue to invest financially in the church, according to the article, "when people see God moving within the church, they will have more faith and be more motivated to give of their finances knowing that it is being sown in good soil." Number thirteen, 'The community isn't impacted.' So, if the church is dying, it not only impacts the power being released in the church but it also impacts the surrounding community. The church should be so in tuned with the power and presence of God that the surrounding community should begin to change for the better, souls should be coming into the kingdom, the crime rate should be going down, not only should the church see miracles and wonders, the community should be blessed by association. We have a long way to go when in the 21st century, we have mass shooters shooting in churches killing multiple people in the middle of a service— and how soon do we forget this, till the next one happens. We should be praying as a body before the shootings occurs. So as a believer if you see any or all of these signs of a dying church, what should you do? Pray, pray and pray some more—seek the face of God for direction. The article even mentioned praying on possibly approaching the leader in a respectful way before making any rash decisions. As a believer, I am at a point in my life where I am in search of more, not the same old program, but a different experience as soon as you enter the sanctuary. I long for the day that the whole church is saturated in the manifested presence of God, and as soon as you walk through the doors, we will be overtaken by the glory of God. If you need salvation, it's done; if you need deliverance, it's done; if you need healing as soon as you enter the doors, it's done; if you need chains broken, they break; if you need deliverance from mental disease, it's done. This is how I envision the church. Yes, I am seeing a picture of the Azusa Street Revival.

The Azusa Street Revival was a historic revival meeting that took place in Los Angeles, California. It was a Pentecostal movement, led by William J. Seymour, an African-American preacher. It started with the first meeting on April 9, 1906, and continued until around 1915. The revival was accompanied by testimonies of physical healing, miracles, worship services which included people speaking in tongues. Some churches do not believe in this today. Some churches believe the gifts are not for the time that we are living in today. Could that be the reason so many churches are either dying, dead or dysfunctional? Even during Azusa, the participants were criticized by the secular media and the Christian theologians. We expect the world, or shall I say, nonbelievers to criticize out of fear of what they do not understand, but the Christian theologians should have known better. We can have all the knowledge and insight in the world about Christianity, but if we do not have that connection to the source that reveals the revelation of God—without the truth, people will not be set free to enjoy a life filled with true purpose. *Mark 16:14-18*: "Later, Jesus appeared to the eleven (disciples) themselves as they were reclining at the table; and He called them to account for their unbelief and hardness of heart, because they had not believed those who had seen Him after He had risen (from death). And He said to them, 'Go into all the world and preach the gospel to all creation. He who has believed (in me) and has been baptized will be saved (from the penalty of God's wrath and judgment); but he who has not believed will be condemned. These signs will accompany those who have believed: In My name they will cast out demons, they will speak in new tongues; they will pick up serpents, and if they drink anything deadly, it will not hurt them; they will lay hands on the sick, and they will get well'."

The Word says for those who believe, there will be some that will be used by God and they will operate in their gifts to the purpose of God. It will be his choice and, in his timing, but for those of you that are willing and ready to be used by God, agreeing is the first step. I pray for the churches that believe the gifts of the spirit are not for this time seek the face of God in search of truth. As Christians, we have to get on one accord and let go of personal agendas and grab hold of God's agenda. I believe so many circumstances would change for the better. The gifts are for this time, to be used strategically, according to the will of God with guidance from the Holy Spirit. The gifts are not to promote the ego of man but the gifts are developed over time, and are used to show the glory of God to the world. *Revelation 2:29 New living translation* says, "Anyone with ears to hear must listen to the Spirit and understand what he is saying to the churches." *Daniel 11:32:* "But the people that do know their God shall be strong, and do exploits." God has given the church a blueprint to follow, that consists of the sword of the Spirit, which is the word of God. *Ephesians 6:17:* "And take The Helmet of Salvation, and the sword of the Spirit, which is the word of God."

The blueprint is not to be changed, misinterpreted nor misrepresented. We cannot add or detract from the blueprint to support our own selfish agendas. So, it is important that we let the Holy Spirit be our guide to train us on how to interpret and follow the blueprint;

without his inspiration we will fall short every time. That's why our relationship with Jesus Christ is so very critical for us to be successful in completing the assignment. If we decide not to follow the blueprint, we will continue to live a defeated life. So as the body of Christ, we have to be willing to follow the blueprint in order to complete the assignment. Or will we go on our own way and follow our own agendas and abandon the assignment to please our flesh? The choice is ours.

I recently went to a prayer meeting with a few of my sisters in Christ, they are all-powerful, beautiful, anointed women of God. I will never forget this particular prayer meeting. We start off every meeting with prayer, and from there, we let the spirit of God do the rest, during this meeting, the host, Melody Jessie, gave a powerful prophetic word that was life-changing for me. "We will see a people that will rise, it will be people that we least expect, people in the background. Prayer changes circumstance and when the change comes, it will come through the church first, then the world. What seems not to be God is God within the confusion. Nations of people will begin to pray; the way we pray will begin to change. God is looking for a people that will not fear or doubt, and take him at his word, no matter how we feel about it. We will have all kinds of critics and we will not always fit in. We will be cast aside, and the fleshly man will begin to feel lonely, but our spirit man will be our comforter in those times of loneliness. We can't be double-minded intercessors, God just wants us to pray, he will give us revelation.

We will have fear, good fear is the reverence of God, and bad fear takes us out of his will. *Job 3:25:* "For the thing which I greatly fear comes upon me, and that of which I am afraid has come upon me." We have to mindful of our thinking—it can cause us to be fearful. Job opened the door to all the stuff that happened to him. We have to be mindful of the thoughts we are thinking. Job's mind became clear and he shut the door to what the enemy had done. God restored him; when you renew your mind, you renew everything within you, but fear causes us to lose sight of the purpose that he has for us. We have to hold those thoughts captive; we can speak life-or-death. (2 Corinthians 10:5-6 AMP) says, "We are destroying sophisticated arguments, and every exalted and proud thing that sets itself up against the (true) knowledge of God, and we are taking every thought and purpose captive to the obedience of Christ, being ready to punish every act of disobedience, when your own obedience (as a church) is complete." (Romans 12:2 NIV) says, "Do not conform to the pattern of this world, but be transformed by the renewing of your mind. Then you will be able to test and approve what God's will is-his good, pleasing and perfect will." So, as I said before, the prophetic words that sister Melody spoke in that meeting on 01/13/2018 are words I will never forget. The Church has to arise and awake from sleeping, and be the powerful body that God has designed it to be. We have to become unified in him and should not be afraid to walk in his power and authority. The church is a giant in Christ Jesus, not in the flesh, not in the world, not in politics but in him. The Church has to become what God intended it to be. "That He might present to Himself the Church in all her glory, having no spot or wrinkle or any such thing; but that she would be holy and blameless." *Ephesians 5:27.*

CHAPTER 4

The church and politics

We were four months into 2018, and I wept one morning after watching the news and seeing the manipulation that the enemy is using against the people of God and the country in general. The people of God must wake up, come out of slumber, and see the truth. We are living in a toxic political environment and as the church, we cannot sell out Christianity for politics and power. We cannot use the Bible to make our political views correct. This would be an example of misrepresenting the blueprint. So, we have to be mindful of how we use the word of God to back up our political beliefs.

I recently read an article from *The Christian Post*, written by *Christian Post* reporter Lillian-Kwon, titled, "An open letter to my black Evangelical friends. Michael Brown conservative host of the nationally syndicated line of fire radio program candidly asks whether black Evangelicals compromised their beliefs by voting for the reelection of President Barack

Obama. He goes on to ask, Are you guilty, on any level, of blind allegiance to the Democratic party? And, on Election Day, did any of you compromise your convictions out of racial solidarity? I simply do not understand how my black evangelical friends who staunchly oppose same-sex marriage, and who stand against abortion could cast their vote for the most radically pro-abortion, pro-gay-activist president in our history. Was there no moral compromise involved in voting for him? Are there no issues that could disqualify him in your eyes? And must Barack Obama be elected and then reelected in order to make up for past injustices, as one black evangelical woman claimed?

He also referenced the 2012 exit polls from the Presidential election in which 93 percent of African-American voters backed Obama, a slight drop from 95% in 2008. Still, an analysis by The New Republic concludes that black turnout or support for Obama might have exceeded 08 levels. Only 6 percent voted for Mitt Romney in 2012.

Turnout among African-Americans steady at 13 percent of the electorate. Brown said he was not attacking black voters in his open letter but that he's simply inquiring why nearly the same percentage of black Americans who voted for Obama in 2008 did so again in 2016. Brown also talked about African-American leaders that made attempts to discourage the African-American community from voting for President Obama in 2012. This article went on to criticize African-

American Christians and question how they could have voted for President Obama twice. One section of the article, written by Mr. Brown's college Bishop, Harry Jackson, stated that, "President Obama has become a personality akin to the biblical figure 'Ishmael' for the

African community instead of the 'child of promise' we had hoped for. In a nutshell, he has attempted to create a new, unbiblical standard of social justice that promotes abortion, same-sex marriage, a distrust of Israel, and a diminishing of religious liberties." When I read the quote that, "President Obama has become a personality akin to the biblical figure 'Ishmael' for the African community." It was very disheartening to read the words from a fellow Christian. For all those who do not know who Ishmael was, read Genesis starting with chapter 16-21. It will give you insight into who Ishmael was. I will let you draw your own conclusion about that statement. I will give you a synopsis of who Ishmael was according to the Word of God. Ishmael was the firstborn son of Abraham and his wife Sarah's Egyptian handmaiden. Since Sarah could not bear children of her own, she insisted Abraham have relations with her handmaiden, so he could have a son. It's pretty safe to say the two women had a complicated relationship. Ishmael around the age of fourteen was sent away with his mother Hagar. God did bless Ishmael and promised to make him fruitful, and multiply him exceedingly and make him a great nation. *Genesis 17:20, Genesis 25:12-16.* Ishmael had 12 sons. If you read the story about Ishmael, you will also find out about

Isaac the second born son of Abraham, conceived by his wife Sarah—now he was the son of promise, not Ishmael. Isaac, the firstborn of Sarah through who came the nation of Israel, the Jewish people and the redeeming Savior of Christ. Ishmael through who came a great nation that represents many, including Arab people—93% of their religious affiliation is Islam. Genesis 16:10-12 says,

"Moreover, the angel of the Lord said to her, 'I will greatly multiple your descendants so that they will be too many to count'. The angel of the Lord said to her further, 'Behold, you are with child, and you will bear a son; and you shall call his name Ishmael, because the Lord has given heed to your affliction. He will be a wild donkey of a man, His hand will be against everyone, and everyone's hand will be against him; and he will live to the east of all his brothers'." So he would always be in conflict. So, you can imagine what I was thinking when I read the quote in the article describing that a Bishop, of all people, compared the first African-American President of the United States to Ishmael—why Ishmael? I begin to think back to what some people said about President Obama—about him not being born in the United States, and making ignorant statements that President Obama is a Muslim instead of a Christian. So of course, knowing the history of Ishmael, I just thought it was interesting for someone to compare President Obama to Ishmael. I wonder if Mr. Brown asked white Evangelicals the same question in 2016 that he asked African-American Christians in 2012;

being that 80 percent of them voted according to statistics for Donald Trump in the 2016 Presidential election. Mr. Browns also went on to say, "In a nutshell, he has attempted to create a new, unbiblical standard of social justice that promotes abortion, same-sex marriage, a distrust of Israel, and a diminishing of religious liberties." I guess those are the reasons African-American Christians should not have voted for President Obama, Mr. Brown did not specifically say African-American Christians should not have voted for President Obama. He instead posed the question and wanted an explanation why.

So would it be fair for African-Americans to asked Mr. Brown and other believers that voted for the current President why and how could you in spite of all the things that were said and done towards women and minorities, not to mention supporting rhetoric that favors racial tensions and policies that continue to uphold systemic racism, policies that benefit the rich and continue to leave the poor and middle class further and further behind.

Would it be fair to say, some Christians may have turned a blind eye to this, in order to regain the political power, they so craved for eight years. Instead of craving political power, we should be striving to obtain the power that dwells within. I also believe that some Christians believed they were voting as per their biblical principles but would this be considered a double standard—in one breath, saying I voted as per my biblical principles, and then ignoring what the Word says about character, love compassion, justice, the poor and many other things. I ask the question: as Christians, where did we go wrong? I often think about whether or not we are doing everything we can as Christians to win souls? We should be praying fervently for the world, putting forth every effort to introduce them to Christ; instead of trying to force people to live according to our beliefs by trying to gain and use political power to force the issue. If we would only do what we have been instructed to do in, *2 Chronicles 7:14*: "If my people, which are called by my name, shall humble themselves, and pray, and seek my face, and turn from their wicked ways; then will I hear from heaven, and forgive their sin, and will heal their land."

If God gives us free will to make our own choices, even on accepting him as our Lord and Savior, then what gives us the right as Christians, to force people through the influence of politics to make choices for their lives. I would pose two more questions to you. As Christians, is our authority greater than God's? Are we wiser than God? Instead of trying to force our will on others, we have to ask God to give us tactics through his Word and prayer, and by his Spirit, to change the heart of man. I have found, over the years, even when dealing with unsaved love ones, if you try to force your values and beliefs on others, you may drive them further away. We have to ask God to search our hearts and make our motives pure. If we are honest with ourselves, no matter how hard we try, we fall short at some point of time in our lives. The Word of God says, "For all have sinned, and fall short of the glory of God." *Romans 3:23*. I am a firm believer that politics can be toxic to the church, and can cause division within the church and between the races. It can become a vehicle the enemy uses to divide and conquer the church, so we have to be so very careful not to get too caught up with the world's systems. I am not saying to totally tune out from what's going on in the world but we cannot allow a dysfunctional political climate to hinder us from doing what's right in the eyes of God. We cannot allow the power of politics to take us off course from God's plan for our lives and for the world. I believe the church has become too consumed when it comes to politics, and if not careful, instead of the church ruling, the political system will begin ruling the church. And this could be a dangerous place to be—in a path filled with strife, pride, racism, division, coldness, mirroring some parts of the world and the political system. The church cannot veer off the path, yes, that path of righteousness. The Church is supposed to be the beacon of light and we are the salt of the earth. *John 12:36-37* says, "'Believe in the light while you have the light, so that you may become children of light'. When he had finished speaking, Jesus left and hid himself from them." *Matthew 5:13* says, "You are the salt of the earth. But if the salt loses its saltiness, how can it be made salty again? It is no longer good for anything, except to be thrown out and trampled underfoot."

We are to lead and be an example for the world not become as the world. The church is supposed to treat people with love, kindness and dignity, regardless of race, creed or color, no matter what their sexual orientation or religious affiliation may be. "Love is patient, love is kind. It does not envy, it does not boast, it is not proud. It does not dishonor others, it is not self-seeking, it is not easily angered, and it keeps no record of wrongs. Love does not delight in evil but rejoices with the truth. It always protects, always trusts, always hopes, and always perseveres. Love never fails. But where there are prophecies, they will cease; where there are tongues, they will be stilled; where there is knowledge, it will pass away." *1 Corinthians 13:4-8.* "Most important of all, continue to show deep love for each other, for love covers a multitude of sins." *1 Peter 4:8.* How far away we are from that quality of love that is described in *1 Corinthians 13:4-8* and *1 Peter 4:8*? When dealing with politics in the Church, why is it that African-American Christians vote overwhelmingly for Democrats and white evangelicals vote overwhelmingly for Republicans? We are all serving the same God, reading the same Word, worshipping and praying to the only wise God. So why are the two races' miles apart when it comes to political affiliation? Could it be that we come from different cultures and backgrounds? Could it be generational—we vote the way our parents voted? Could it be because of the history of the country and race relations?White evangelicals play a major role in the Republican Party, and Christians of color play a major role in the Democratic Party, so if we are all believers of the same body, why are we so divided? Could it be because of the history of our country that still comes between us even though we are supposed to be brothers and sisters in Christ. It always seems to be race that comes in between us—that huge elephant in the room. I would hope, as Christians, each one of us would pray that God will open our eyes to the truth, that each of us would examine ourselves deep down on the inside in search of the truth. I firmly believe the election of the first African-American played a huge roll in the aftermath of the 2016 election. We must face hard facts and ask God to remove the blinders from our eyes, so we can see the truth, and not our truth but THE TRUTH. "Jesus told him, 'I am the way, the truth, and the life. No one can come to the Father except through me'." *John 14:6* What is the key to seeing and knowing the truth? The only way to know his truth, is by developing a close relationship with THE TRUTH, Jesus Christ. I believe the election of the first black President was turned into something sinister and dark that started with the conservative movement known to us as the tea party movement. If we are being honest, we would ask if the war cry from this conservative tea party movement was truly just against the policies of the first African-American President? Or did race play a part in the strong rebuke against President Obama? I am curious to know why some Christians say they voted against President Obama because they were voting for their biblical principles. How does voting biblical principles line up with the current administration's actions? Support continues even after all of the chaos released upon our country. There is continued support even after seeing what has happened since the 2016 election—starting with everything that we have witnessed in the first year, including what happened in Charlottesville, the march of white supremacist, white nationalist, neo-confederates, Klansmen, neo-Nazis and various militias, with the protesters chanting racist and anti-Semitic slogans to oppose the removal of a statue of Robert E. Lee from Emancipation Park. The case for voting for biblical principles seems like a hypocritical argument in this moment in time. It was very painful to hear the President of the United States say that there were good people on both sides; so, I would ask the question again, if we are serving the same God, why are we so far apart politically?

Now let's look at policies of both parties, and how they line up with biblical principles. The Republican Party is supposed to be the party of the right wing. According to dictionary.com right wing is, "members of a conservative or reactionary political party, or those opposing extensive political reform. That part of a political or social organization advocating a conservative or reactionary position:" The Republican Party was known for being the party of fiscal responsibility, paying down the debt of the country, and balancing the budget. Fiscal responsibility was so very important to conservatives when President

Obama was in office, now that we have a new President in Washington, fiscal responsibility is a term that has no business being used by either party. The Democratic Party is known to be more liberal, the party of the left. According to the dictionary left wing means, "members of a liberal or radical political party, or those favoring extensive political reform; the part of a political or social organization advocating a liberal or radical position." I will take it even further and say the Republican Party has a reputation of being morally right and conservative on issues regarding abortion and the sanctity of marriage along with immigration.

I once heard that Republicans believe in pulling yourself up by your own bootstraps and improving your situation by your own efforts without the help of others. They don't believe or care for social programs or receiving a handout. The Republicans are known for looking out for big corporations and big banks. They support an open and free market with fewer regulations, believing the wealth will trickle down but we know that idea is bogus.

The Democratic Party is known as the party that believes more in social programs to help the poor and the less fortunate. But sometimes, instead of helping, their policies have often led to a lifetime of enabling individuals, keeping them in the same cycle of bondage and poverty. They appear to be on the side of justice and equal rights for all people. I do believe that they fight harder for the rights of all people but I also believe there should be some reform when it comes to immigration and social programs; providing more programs of training to help people find better opportunities. The Democratic Party is known for supporting women's rights, and even though I am a born-again believer, and I do not believe in abortion, I do believe that we have choices that we have to make for our own lives. I pray that each person deciding will choose life but that decision is for each woman to make—all we can do as Christians is pray and not judge. "Do not judge, or you too will be judged. For in the same way you judge others, you will be judged, and with the measure you use, it will be measured to you." *Matthew 7: 1-2*

I read an interesting article written by Todd Strandberg, and it was titled, 'Would Jesus vote Republican?' He started off by talking about the politics of Rome during the time of Jesus, and went on to say, it was simple and to the point—either you followed the law of Caesar or dissented and were killed. He went on to say, "You could live in peace, that is, unless you came into conflict with the pious Jews who used the Law of Moses like a battering ram to get their own way, and keep themselves in sub-authority just beneath the occupying Romans. Jesus was railroaded to trial by the malicious use of just such religious politics." I thought to myself after reading that paragraph, wow, that sounds familiar.

He also touched on how politics has not changed that much over time, as far as the structure in which to elect leaders for the government to make our society peaceful and also to maintain some form of order, is concerned. "It is more often than not, a wicked instrumentality with which to bludgeon anyone and everyone who might have differing opinions. In short, the political process is the end-justifies-the-means way to achieve power over others." The writer went on to quote Lord Acton's remark, "Power corrupts; absolute power corrupts absolutely." We have to ask ourselves, are we letting the corruption of politics seep into the church? The good news is, there is still time to stop the leak. The writer went on to say, "One of the ironic things about tyranny is that it does not need to be maintained. Once a nation falls into totalitarianism, it's no small task to regain liberty. Democracy, on the other hand, needs constant care because the beliefs and values of the press, religions, and private citizens often conflict with the policies of the governments that represent them, a system of checks and balances is needed to maintain freedom. Because the enemies of liberty are ever on the offensive, Christians don't have the option of walking away from the political battlefield. Liberalism has already gained an advantage by taking over the schools, media and many denominations. Because believers are neglecting to become involved in politics, the enemy continues to use the political process to manipulate and herd America into ungodliness; unopposed, that tyrannical power will ultimately enslave us." I thought that this was a very interesting statement; for one, America has been engulfed in ungodliness from the beginning, shall we begin with Native Americans in 1776 when the United States begin seizing land from North America's native people; or the ungodly act of slavery in America that began in the 1619. Yes, as Christians, we do have to get involved and be a part of making decision on who would be better to represent our communities. As Christians, we also have the responsibility to mirror the image of Christ not the world. His image is his character. As Christians, we should be craving to be more like him. So, we do have to be very careful that in all our passion in trying to do the right thing, we do not end up doing our own thing. We do not want to fall short of mirroring the image of God. "And we all, with unveiled face, continually seeing as in a mirror the glory of the Lord, are progressively being transformed into His image from (one degree of) glory to (even more) glory, which comes from the Lord, (who is) the Spirit." *2 Corinthians 3:18.*

We may be fighting in our own eyesight for a righteous cause but do we seek the face of God for direction in every situation? "There is a way which seems right to a man, but its end is the way to death." *Proverbs 14:12.*

The article went on to discuss why the Lord would certainly not be a Democrat, "There is one thing certain we can state, based upon the integrity of Bible truth. Jesus would never endorse or be a member of any party whose platform supports abortion, gay rights, and a general hostility to Bible-believing Christians. Another thing can be confidently stated, based upon observation of current facts about American politics. The Democrat Party would never have Jesus as a member. Much of the basis for that observation is found in the issues mentioned above. The Democrats' leadership consistently supports abortion—or, as they term it— "the right to choose." They continue to support homosexual activities and their "gay rights" causes—a debased, debauched lifestyle that God calls abominable. Democrats defend pornography as art that comes under the heading of "free speech." After reading this section of the article, I thought to myself, he seems to have all the answers as to what all Democrats are thinking, and what they would do in every circumstance. He assumes that everyone that votes democratically is a sinner and cannot possibly be a believer, or love Jesus just as much as the Evangelical Republican does. Speaking of love, he did not once mention the love of Christ in the above argument of why Jesus could never be a member of the Democratic Party. I could not help but wonder if the author was one of the eighty percent of Evangelical Christians that voted for the Republican candidate in the 2016 Presidential election. I wonder if he compromised his values and biblical principles to vote Republican in the 2016 Presidential election. He went on to say, "This political party comes down on the side of liberal federal judges who have ruled that God should be thrown out of the public places of America. These judges and the Democratic Party by supporting them—declare "The

Ten Commandments," "In God We Trust" on our currency, and "One nation, under God" in the "Pledge of Allegiance" dangerous to our school children and our society."

As a Christian myself, I do believe taking God out of the schools and public places was a huge mistake, if we look at where we are today with all the chaos in the world, the mass shootings in the schools, the bigotry, injustices against people of color, and all of the corruption and divisiveness. But to say that all Democrats supported the Supreme Court's decision in 1962-1963 to remove the Bible and prayer from our public schools would be misleading. He quoted the part in the Pledge of Allegiance, "One nation, under God" to make his point. If given the opportunity to have a conversation with the writer, I would ask him to take a second look at the Pledge of Allegiance, and pay special attention to the part that says, "With liberty and justice for all." Then determine if it would be fair to say that Republicans do not believe in the notion of liberty and justice for all because they supported the right-wing justices that decided the 2013 decision of the Supreme Court to invalidate key parts of the Voting Rights Act. It would be wrong of me to speculate that all Republicans are the same. We have to make a conscious effort not to judge one another when it comes to our political beliefs, and not assume everyone believes and thinks the same way. Just because an individual is affiliated with one party versus the other, does not give us the right to judge that person's character and pretend to know where they stand on every issue. The writer blames the Democratic party and Democratic President for being first at taking trillions of taxpayers' money from the pockets of those who work to give to those who won't work, even if they have opportunity; He refers to this as, violating a basic precept of God's word (2 Thess, 3:10) says,

"For even when we were with you, this we commanded you, that if any would not work, neither should he eat." My response to that is it is not that simple, and he is not taking into consideration the systematic and social economic racism that's buried so deep into this country. I believe we do have a major problem in this country with poverty and the welfare system, and the system does need to be revamped in a way to increase the quality of life for those individuals that have been left behind, by giving them greater opportunities.

I also believe that most of the people that are on the system actually need the help. But there will always be a small percent of the people of all races on the system that should not be; those individuals are taking advantage of the system and need to be held accountable. I also believe that there are also individuals that have been receiving assistance for so long that they have become dependent on the system and they do not know how to become financially free. Most of us have dealt with financial hardship in one form or another, such as the loss of a job, the loss of one income in a two-income household secondary to the development of an illness or disability, the death of a spouse, a single parent trying very hard to make it by working two or three jobs. The system was not meant to become a long-term crutch or to be used as a long-term source of income for people that are able to work. I believe this is where the Democratic Party gets it wrong. I believe the government should invest more of our tax dollars into education and healthcare and proper housing, providing avenues so all of our kids and communities can have a fair shake at having a better life and more opportunities, instead of investing in the rich and large corporations and special interest groups. As a country, we need to invest more in our small businesses, especially black-owned businesses that struggle more than most businesses. I believe this is where the Republican Party gets it wrong.

I am a firm believer that the elderly and disabled population should always be taken care of. I have seen both sides of the argument due to the field that I work in. I work with some individuals that do depend on the system for assistance, and for the most part, I agree with helping people with those basic needs. Most people that find themselves in this predicament are actually working very hard to better themselves but we do see a small percentage of individuals that get caught up in the system, and they get comfortable in that state. I really believe, this is a form of continued bondage and oppression that began when the first slaves stepped off of the ship in Virginia in 1619. I truly believe that those individuals that become trapped in this generational cycle are dealing with a state of bondage in their mind. The cycle of poverty and their environment has trained them to accept and believe that this is it. I believe the mindset of those individuals has to be changed to make them believe that yes, they can do better, and they can strive for more for themselves and their family. "I can do all things through Christ who strengthens me." *Philippians 4:13*.

As a country, we should be assisting and encouraging the next generation to make a change and break the cycle of poverty and dependence on the system. We have to assist them in obtaining the tools to become financially independent, whether that's training for a higher paying career and or the opportunity to invest in them to help them become entrepreneurs. I know everyone has dreams and talents; why not as a country, invest in those dreams and the talents of others, instead of keeping people oppressed and in bondage? Once they are financially free, this in turn will be good for them and the country. Trust me when I say, once you have experienced some level of success through and by hard work and trusting God, it will make all the difference in the world.

I know some of you may be wondering if this is firsthand knowledge. The answer would be, yes, I was a teenage single mother, raised mainly by my mother in a low-income neighborhood after my father left when I was around six or seven years old. I grew up seeing young, single women having multiple children with the fathers in and out of the household, never being trained to answer the call and be there for the children that they helped to bring into the world. Yes, it is a vicious cycle—a cycle that still exists in many communities today... a cycle that has to be broken. I am living proof that the cycle can be broken. I had my first son two months before my eighteenth birthday but I thank God that he put a drive inside me. I wanted more for myself and my son, so I finished school, received my diploma, and I used the opportunities offered and went on to get a degree and became a Registered Nurse. I thank God for the desire he placed within me to want a better life for me and my son, and not to depend on a broken system that is a big part of the systematic racism, to take care of us. I also had a supportive mother, who constantly prayed for us. He also sent me a wonderful husband, who is also in the medical field. We have to let the next generation know that they can do better in the face of adversity. With much prayer, encouragement, the proper resources, motivation and determination, any goal can be obtained.

In my field of work, I have had the opportunity to see the vicious cycle of oppression and lack of motivation, with broken children raising children. The system can be a blessing and a curse at the same time. Blessing as far as taking care of the elderly and disabled, or a family that is in temporary need of support, secondary to loss of income for whatever reason, or a single mother in school needing temporary relief to aid with medical insurance and daycare for her children, or a family working hard to make ends meet but is falling short and needs that additional assistance until they get back on their feet. In the above circumstances, the individuals are doing everything they can to better their situation but can use a helping hand.

The system can become a curse for individuals that feel like they are stuck in this system of oppression. The system can often become a hindrance to a person's progress, if it is not managed properly, often doing more harm than good. Being caught up in the system can cause generational oppression and more crime. I am convinced that opportunity is the key to fixing a broken system. I know this is a difficulty topic of discussion, especially in the African-American community, but it is a discussion that we must have, if we want to see things change for the better. People do what they know and know what they see—someone has to break the cycle. We pray that God will break the yoke of bondage. "It shall come about on that day, declares the LORD of hosts, 'that I will break his yoke from off their neck and will tear off their bonds; and strangers will no longer make them slaves'." *Jeremiah 30:8.* As a people, we can be enslaved in our minds when it comes to our hopes and dreams. If we continue to think negatively about our circumstances, it can have a detrimental impact on our future. We have to change our way of thinking.

The aforementioned writer went on to discuss why Jesus would not be a Republican, "We can say with equal certainty that Jesus would not be a card-carrying member of the Republican party. The Grand Old Party may share many values that can be traced back to the Bible, but it is still the GOP, not the GOD party. Because the party is run by corrupt man, a perfect and Holy God would never lend His credibility to that or any other earthly organization. The Republican Party has been branded by the Democrats to be the "party of greed." This label is not stamped without a degree of legitimacy.

Man is a greedy being in his fallen state. Politicians within both major parties use the love of money to step on the backs of those they are supposed to serve. There are few innocent of power-grabbing for riches within the American political process. When it gets down to the bare facts, the only advantage the Republican party offers is that it is the lesser of two evils." I certainly agree with most of what the writer said in the last paragraph, that with politics, comes a certain degree of evil and corruption in both parties. I would not want to be that closed-minded and say that every politician is evil and corrupt. But I do believe we are living in a climate where things are much worse. The political climate in the country is very divisive at this point, and no, I do not believe the Republican party is the lesser of two evils. There is good and evil on both sides, that's why, as Christians, we have to pray for both parties, the entire political arena. Another part of the article that I thought was interesting and very true was, "humanism remains at the core of the GOP's, or any party's attempts to rule. This means that it, like its Democratic counterpart, is fatally flawed. To be specific, sin reigns supreme within its ranks because human beings, most wanting to see their star rise above all other stars, as often as not throw character and integrity aside to achieve goals—usually of a self-serving nature. Again, ends justify means in the political process." I totally agree with the writer on the above issue, especially in the season we are currently living in, both parties have pushed the truth and common decency out of the window. How can a divided house be successful? Well, I will give you the answer to that question. IT CAN'T. And that is why, the country is in the state that it is currently in. If the leadership from both parties fail to come together for the good of the country to help make people's lives better, then they should rethink their career choice. If the average person who was employed could not effectively do his/her job, it would be time for them to move on. As Christians, we have to keep praying for Washington that God will send individuals that are willing to serve the people with integrity and compassion, individuals that are not willing to sell their soul for rich donors and power. We pray that God will send people to represent us with his heartbeat. I believe the writer had some valid points and very strong views. Once again, we have to be very careful with mixing Christianity and politics. If we are not careful, we can be in too deep, and start to compromise ourselves and our values without even knowing we have done so.

I recently read another interesting blog written in March of 2016, by Pastor Matthew Walker, titled, 'Politics in the end times.' I would like to take the time to share some points of the article with you. Pastor Walker starts off describing some political rally in America, some of the rhetoric that is hurled at the people and the message of politics and social issues that he brings to the people.

He speaks about economic growth, about immigration policy, about what's wrong in the government. He does not give many solutions to these perceived problems, but he offers up himself as the answer. His speech has reference to the Bible and to God, though it is apparent that people who identify as evangelical are supporting his candidacy in record numbers. If enough people vote for him, he will take his place as the next leader of the world.

The writer went on to say, "This is not a description of the 2016 Republican presidential primary, even if some parallels appear in the story between the two." This is a fictional account of the election of the Antichrist, the political figure who will arise at some point in the future according to God's perfect timing. This man is described in a few places and in the Bible—*Ezekiel 28, Daniel 7, 2 Thessalonians 2,* and *Revelation 13* and *17*. Look at how *2 Thessalonians 2* describes this man. In 2:3, he is called "the man of sin"; 2:4, he opposes God and desires worship (notice the connection between politics and religion), in 2:9, his power is Satanic and so very deceptive that even Christians will be tempted to believe him). 2:11, he will deceive unbelievers. "Think about this coming election. In some form of future global democracy, the people of the world will rise up and support this man who opposes God and even people who call themselves Christians will support him." The writer made another excellent point, about the only way to know how a person will behave in office is too, "judge his words according to what he has already done. If a person has advocated practices which are immoral in the past, his present-day commitment to morality must be questioned. Second, this highlights the importance of recognizing the influence of Satan upon the political system." I wanted to share some points of this article with you because I believe it was dead on. We have seen so much during this last election cycle, and politics can become overwhelming if we allow it to saturate our state of mind. As Christians, we all have overruled some things about a candidate's personality and or policies that we may have not totally agreed on. But you go with that candidate because you feel they will be the best person to represent the people's interest.

After the 2016 Presidential election, we all have heard Christians say, "I voted according to my biblical principles." I thought to myself exactly what does voting as per your biblical principles mean? Does it mean no matter what, we are supposed to vote Republican because they are the conservative righteous party? What exactly does that saying mean? So, of course, I have another interesting article that will really make you think when it comes to being a Christian and voting: 'Voting with a Christian conscience' by Dr. Erwin W. Lutzer.

Dr. Lutzer writes about the fact that he believes the evangelical church was finally forced to conclude that the church cannot depend on politics to turn the country around, nor bring us back to biblical principles, or reverse the anti-Christian bigotry developing in the courts, the media, and the wider culture. I agree with him one hundred percent when he states, "Only the church, armed with the Gospel, is able to bring lasting change in the hearts and lives of people. God's House—and not the White House—holds the key to the future of our nation." He also discusses the fact that it was time for the Church to stand tall without the support of the political leaders, and the fact that over time, God has allowed good and bad leaders. Some were a perfect fit for the people but some were not, but regardless of the leader, the church must remain faithful to its calling. He also went on to say he did not endorse political candidates because, no one candidate is right on all the issues, or for that matter, wrong on all the issues, and the Gospel should never be tied to a politician or political party. We should never give the impression that one party or another is the "Christian party." We must be able to say to Democrats, Republicans, and Independents and everyone between, that unless you believe in Jesus, you will be eternally separated from God."

The article had much more information, and I recommend that you go back and read the entire piece. It gave me clarity. I am not saying that it is wrong for them to vote as per their biblical principles. But does that, in turn, mean that it is a rule that you vote for the same party, no matter what? For instance, it was maybe around five years ago when the Democratic Party in my state elected a self-proclaimed atheist, and even though his policies seemed to be in line with helping the average citizen, I could not vote for him because of my faith. As a Christian there are certain lines that we should not cross regardless of party affiliation. In both parties, there are certain policies I agree with and can relate to, as well as policies on both sides that I do not agree with. There have been times in my life when I have voted for the opposite party. I voted for a Republican multiple times in the past because I could relate to his message, and I believed he was a man of integrity and he made some valid points. He would send out emails to his constituents to get our opinion on different issues that he would have to vote on. I did have prior knowledge of his voting record, and no, I did not agree with him on all of his policies but I felt like he was a person that I could trust as far as his character and his belief in prayer spoke for him. So yes, it is ok to cross party lines even if you are a Christian.

We have to learn to trust more in God rather than putting our trust in man to do what only God can do. *Psalm 62:8:* "Trust (confidently) in Him at all times, O people; pour out your heart before Him. God is a refuge for us." Sometimes, as Christians, we want to cherry-pick from the Word—yes, pick and choose what parts of the Word we are going to follow. Most Christians will pinpoint abortion and same-sex marriage as being the reason why they affiliate with the Republican Party. So, as Christians, do we ignore everything else about a candidate—their character and who and what they are connected to? For instance, in Virginia, in 2018, the Republican Party elected a candidate, who in the past, has called a white Nationalist named Paul Nehlen his hero.

According to the *Huffington Post*, "piggybacking off reporting from the site Angry White Men, which monitors the activity of white supremacists-documented Nehlen's history of making racist and anti-Semitic posts on Twitter and Gab, a social media platform used primarily by racists and fascists." Nehlen's racist rhetoric on twitter caused Twitter to permanently suspend his account." The candidate also expressed support for the white supremacists who marched at the deadly "Unite the Right" rally in Charlottesville, Virginia, where a neo-Nazi allegedly drove his car into a crowd of counter-protesters, killing antiracist activist Heather Heyer "and that is not even the tip of the iceberg. So it is beyond me to fathom how this candidate could not have known the character of the man he so quickly called his hero. The candidate did later report that he had cut ties with Nehlen, and he no longer considered him his hero after learning about the crazy things Nehlen had been saying. However, even with that being said, it is just hard for me to believe he had no idea about the major character flaw in the man that he called his hero. What does this say about the candidate's character and judgment in this day and time?

I also saw this candidate on a media network on August 18, 2018 I remember this day well, as this was my birthday. He was on the show discussing whether the President of the United States was a racist—so sad. He talked about how the left -wing media interjected race into every topic. But what shook me to my core was the fact that he said they were back in the 60s, and how the country has moved on from racial issues. It was kind of scary to hear a Senate candidate from my home state, Virginia, actually stating that people nationally and in the state of Virginia do not care about race anymore. He actually claimed that the African Americans he had talked to in his community did not believe that race was a major concern in our country. I can tell you from firsthand knowledge, as an African American woman who has lived in the state of Virginia all of my life, that statement is far from the truth. If a poll was conducted in his district of Prince County in Virginia asking African Americans if racial inequality still exists, the answer would be 'absolutely yes'. So it was a big concern for me that this man could have the power if elected to change and make new laws that could impact my life and the lives of my children without having any real awareness of how racial inequality in our country affects millions of us today. And for me, that is a scary thought. But what was more concerning to me is that this candidate with ties to white nationalists received 44.78 percent of the vote.

As Christians, we all should have a certain measure of discernment to help us to distinguish between good and evil. It is a major tool of warfare. Our measure of discernment often depends on how developed our personal relationship is with the Trinity. If you are a Christian and you feel that you may need another level of discernment, you have a right to go straight to the source and ask for whatever you need and if you need to be filled with his spirit, just ask. *1 Corinthians 2:14* says, "The person without the Spirit does not accept the things that comes from the Spirit of God but considers them foolishness, and cannot understand them because they are discerned only through the Spirit."*1 John 4:1:* "Dear friends, do not believe every spirit, but test the spirits to see whether they are from God, because many false prophets have gone out into the world". 1King 3:9: "So give your servant a discerning heart to govern your people and to distinguish between right and wrong. For who is able to govern this great people of yours?"

In closing, as a Christian, it does not matter if you consider yourself a Democrat or a Republican, because both political parties have had a certain level of corruption over the years. It cannot be our motto, as Christians, to win by any means necessary, even if it takes lying, cheating, stealing, withholding the truth, turning a blind eye to wrongdoing. Therefore, as Christians, we have to truly seek the face of God for direction, even when it comes to casting our votes for either party. We can no longer just say that we are voting according to our biblical principles, and at the same time, support flagrant corruption and lies that are so bold and obvious that you can clearly see the Puppet Master—yes, the enemy behind the scenes—pulling the strings, and creating the chaos. It is so critical that as believers we begin to learn how to see through our spiritual eyes and hear through our spiritual ears in this season so we will not be deceived. *Numbers 24:4:* "The oracle of him who hears the words of God, who sees the vision of the Almighty, falling down, yet having his eyes uncovered." *2 Kings 6:17:* "Then Elisha prayed and said, 'O LORD, I pray, open his eyes that he may see.' And the LORD opened the servant's eyes and he saw; and behold, the mountain was full of horses and chariots of fire all around Elisha."

CHAPTER 5

The truth will set you free

A couple of months ago, I read an interesting post on Facebook written by Bruce Horst. He started out saying that he lost his Christianity over healthcare reform (Obamacare). He talked about how, for the majority of his adult life, he was self-employed. He also described himself as an overweight man with a family history of heart disease, adding that he was uninsurable. He could afford health insurance but no insurance company would cover him—not even at a higher cost—probably because he was overweight with a family history of heart disease. He tried for many years to buy health insurance but was denied. Bruce was self-employed for many years, and according to him, made a lot of money. But as we all know; money doesn't solve all our problems. According to Bruce he also lost a lot of sleep over worrying about what would happen to him and his family if he was to get sick, and for whatever reason, had to be hospitalized. He knew that one surgery and a few nights in a hospital would wipe out all of his life savings, and that would lead to him having difficulty paying for his kid's college education and his retirement.

He also said in his post, "For all those that say or think America takes care of our poor through emergency room care, they are mistaken because no one is able to get surgery in the emergency or nor do they give people chemotherapy for cancer in an emergency room." I would go on to say that in the emergency room, they do the bare minimal for people that are not insured. Bruce said in his post that in 2010, he had been a conservative evangelical Christian for all of his adult life, and he began to realize that the people around him did not want people like him to benefit from the affordable health insurance because they believed it would put them at a disadvantage.

When I read some of Bruce's comments, I knew more than ever that every person is entitled to have good affordable healthcare. As Christians, we are supposed to have compassion for others because of the Christ within us. Shouldn't we want the best for our fellowmen or is it ok for us to just think and care about our own lives and families? As Christians, when we speak the truth, we have to speak the whole truth. Once again, we cannot cherry-pick the Word of God to suit our own ideas and opinions. We are supposed to want the best for one another, and hold others in higher esteem than ourselves. *Philippians 2:3* says, "Let nothing be done through strife or vainglory; but in lowliness of mind, let each esteem other better than themselves." So that tells me that we are supposed to look out for others that are less fortunate than us.

In this post, Bruce said something so profound, "As a Christian, I believed that I would be judged on the final Judgment Day on how I took care of the least of these' as described in the Bible Book of Matthew, Chapter 25. I came to the sober realization that Christians around me had no such convictions. If they didn't believe Jesus' words as recorded in the Bible, why should I? Then one day, I discovered I could no longer believe any of it. That was six and a half years ago, and today I'm more comfortable in my position in life than I've ever been. I still have a lot of Evangelical friends, but I can say with confidence that the vast majority of them are not followers of Jesus. Not the Jesus the Bible speaks of, anyway." He went on to talk about the plans that Congress had for Obamacare to take away health insurance for more than 18 million of Americans, and they will be doing this upon the insistence of Conservative Christians.

After I read this post, I came to the realization that once again, as Christians, sometimes we want to pick and choose what we are going to follow in God's word, as it pertains to our views but as we begin to develop a true relationship with Jesus Christ, he will show us a better way. *John 14:6* says, "Jesus answered, 'I am the way and the truth and the life. No one comes to the Father except through me'."

The Christians that Bruce is referring to are ones that are pro-life when it comes to abortions but often are against every American having good health insurance, in order to stay healthy and to sometimes save lives by way of receiving lifesaving treatments such as chemotherapy and insulin therapy, dialysis—all treatments needed to sustain life. If they are pro-life, it seems that they would want everyone to have access to affordable health insurance to be able to sustain life; so once again, this appears to be a double standard because all life matters. Just food for thought. Sometimes we feel that because we are Christians, we have the right to be judge and jury, and act on the behalf of God, but we have to realize that God doesn't need us to do his job for him. However, he does need us to be wise representatives for his kingdom, making sure that he is seen through us. Once again, he gives each and every one us free will, even when it comes to receiving and accepting him into our hearts. So, with that being said, what makes us think that we can force people to make choices that we would make for our own lives.

Where are we as a country today? In the first quarter of 2017, I would say, in a state of emergency. We have a party of majority men in charge of making life decisions that will impact millions of Americans by attempting to take away healthcare from millions of people. Only three Republican Senators stood up for what is right, and we have to give credit where credit is due. This fiscal conservative bunch also approved a huge tax cut that will mostly benefit the wealthy and do very little for the poor, middle class and small businesses; willing to sacrifice the poor and struggling Americans to make the rich richer and the poor poorer. Where is the compassion? May 4 2017 is when the steps began to be taken towards repealing and replacing the affordable healthcare, in which would include taking healthcare away from millions of people, along with raising the cost for millions of more people with pre-existing conditions. My family would be included in that number. My eldest son is currently receiving Obamacare and I was diagnosed with a condition called lupus over 3 years ago. I have been healthy most of my life. I exercised on a routine basis, had no problems with hypertension, heart disease or diabetes. My job as a Registered Nurse for more than twenty years has allowed me the chance to take care of many sick people, which included my mother up until her death. I also have a brother that lost his sight shortly after our mother passed away because he was unable to afford the expensive medicine, he needed to manage glaucoma. He did have insurance at the time through his employer but unfortunately the insurance wasn't the best. A couple of years after he went blind, he developed kidney failure, and in order for him to even receive dialysis, he would have to come up with a two-thousand-dollar co-pay even though he has some insurance. Yes, I know what you must be thinking—that is ridiculous. My brother's wife also has a diagnosis of multiple sclerosis, and their daughter was born with Down syndrome. No, I am not making this up—it is true—all true!

What our government is attempting to do is putting all Americans in jeopardy. So, of course I have reason to be concerned. I believe if the leaders in charge who are making all the critical decisions for all of us had to walk one year in the shoes of the people who are struggling to make it, in addition to being a caregiver for a loved one who has a disability or illness, and at the same time figuring out how to pay medical bills and still keep a roof over their heads, maybe… just maybe… our leaders would have a little more compassion for the less fortunate. This is the reality, and some of the struggle for many of the elderly and disabled people needing additional resources in order to survive. This is the reality for most caregivers who still have to work and provide for their own families while still having the responsibility of taking care of an elderly and sometimes disabled parent. Believe me, I have been on both sides. So, I know how hard it can be to try to make sure that your loved one is taken care of. I am also included in the list of millions of other individuals who are considered to have a preexisting condition. We did not ask for the diagnosis, we can't trade in our genetic makeup, and we can't control the environment or the chemicals and toxins that are being put in the foods today. We can only make a conscious effort to do all we can to live healthy lives, and continue to pray for our total and complete healing.

As Christians, we all have an opportunity to receive healing because Jesus already paid the price for us to receive healing by the stripes he endured on the cross. We all know that *Isaiah 53:5* says, "But He was wounded for our transgressions; He was bruised for our iniquities; the chastisement for our peace was upon Him, and by His stripes, we are healed." That healing can come through medicine and technology. I am living witness of that fact. When I was first diagnosed with lupus, the doctors tried a couple of different treatments to combat all the symptoms that were attacking my body. I had crippling pain in my joints along with massive amounts of swelling in my hands, so much so that it was a task for me to even pump gas or use my hand to dress myself. It even impacted me at work, as far as being able to complete certain tasks, such as squeezing the bulb to inflate the blood pressure cuff, were concerned. I just remember it being so painful and the only way I could complete the task was by using both hands. Could you imagine having to pace yourself while walking to avoid having to deal with shortness of breath? It was only through prayer and the blood of Jesus that I was able to perform my job and make it through the day.

When I was first diagnosed, I had insurance through my husband's employer because I was self-employed. The insurance we had at that time was excellent, so it covered mostly all my medicines and visits to my rheumatologist with a reasonable co-pay. A year into my diagnosis, my husband's employer decided to change the healthcare plan to another insurer who only offered junk plans where we had to satisfy an enormous deductible before the insurance company would pay. So, you can imagine the stress this caused me when my husband first informed me of the change. In this life, we will always have trials and tribulations but the beauty of it is when you have a relationship with Jesus Christ, something deep down on the inside will arrest your spirit long enough to give you a peace in your circumstance. I believe the Word calls that thing that's deep down on the inside of every born-again believer, 'The Hope of Glory'. I know some of you who don't know are asking, what does she mean? Or what is she referring to? For all of you who don't know, the Hope of Glory means that Christ in us is the Hope of Glory. "God has chosen to make known among the Gentiles, the glorious riches of this mystery, which is Christ in you, the hope of glory.": *Colossians 1:27.* For all of you who do know the truth, you should be getting your praise on right now! So once that Hope of Glory connected with my spirit through in by his spirit, I knew that I had to trust God and continue to pray, and that's exactly what I did. If you are a believer then you should know the outcome, yes, of course, he answered my prayer.

Let me tell you the story of how he did it, it's going to blow your mind. *Romans 8:28* says, "And we know that all things work together for good to them that love God, to them who are the called according to his purpose." Let me tell you how I know the Word is true. Well, the blessings began when the company that my husband worked for lost their contract with a major nursing and rehab center, where they provided physical therapy services. I would like to take this time to be honest with you and tell you that when I first received the news, I didn't know what to make of it. So, I did the only thing I knew to do, and that was to fall down on my knees and pray. And a couple days later, my husband informed me that the company that was canceling his employer's contract had offered him a full-time position with a significant pay increase and with better insurance, and this in turn, led me back to the specialist who had treated me at first, and eventually, led me to the Supreme blessing—my healing through and by a new drug used to treat lupus. Now let me tell you about the blessing within the blessing: the cost of this drug that I received once a month through IV infusion was over three thousand dollars, and my current insurance paid all of the cost except forty dollars a month. God is just that good. He took an impossible situation and turned it around for my good, so the Word is absolutely true. The doctor said at my last appointment that according to my lab results, there was no trace of lupus in my body, and I have been asymptomatic for over two years now. So, believe me when I say there are no limits to what God can do.

If you are a child of God, it's so very important not to doubt him, no matter what your situation looks like because looks can be deceiving. *Mark 11:23* says, "Truly, I say to you, whoever says to this mountain, be taken up and thrown into the sea, and does not doubt in his heart, but believes that what he says will come to pass, it will be done for him." *Romans 12:12:* "Constantly rejoicing in hope (because of our confidence in Christ), steadfast and patient in distress, devoted to prayer (continually seeking wisdom, guidance, and strength).

I am a prime example of why it is so very vital that each and every individual in this country has adequate health insurance. So, if you are a believer, I would ask that you go deep down on the inside of your spirit to that place where the Hope of Glory dwells (the Christ inside of you), and pull from that source to obtain insight on who to support when it comes to healthcare. Will you make a conscious effort to follow the word and look out for the poor and the less fortunate or will you be a part of that tribalism that is rooted so deep into our political system? It was May 22, 2017, when the administration's proposed budget plan for 2018 included cutting Medicaid and food stamps by 800 billion over the coming decade. Who would that affect the most? The elderly, disabled and children living in poverty. How is that for compassion? But in the same breath, our current leaders want to give big tax cuts to the rich while trying to fool the middle class into thinking that this is in our best interests.

To tell you the truth, this is not shocking to hear, but what is shocking to me is the silence of some of the leaders in the church. The

Bible says, the poor will always be among us so once again I will ask, does that same Bible teach us to turn our backs on the poor and the less fortunate? No, it says the opposite. So thank God that all these decisions that need to be made during this time are in his hands and I am so thankful that he is faithful regarding his promises. I don't want to judge anyone because I have made so many mistakes in my life that God has forgiven me for, and none of us have arrived, so we cannot cast stones at one another. I know all of the above is true, and I believe it from the bottom of my heart, and I know if I continue to seek the face of God, he will give me the insight that I so desperately seek and the mindset not to stand in judgment of others. Even when I do not understand some of the decisions that have been made by some our leaders that are professed Christians that could have a lasting impact on the wellbeing of others...

When hearts and minds are in turmoil, and we see things in the world that are so clearly wrong, what do we do? We continue to go back to the source, 'the Hope of Glory' over and over again. In this season, we have to constantly seek God for direction, guidance and understanding. I pray: Lord, help me to see people as you see them with love and compassion even when it seems impossible to do so. Even though this world we live in often looks bleak at times, we have to make a conscious effort to look beyond what we see. When I see the world in disarray, I go back to *Isaiah 41:10:* "So do not fear, for I am with you; do not be dismayed, for I am your God. I will strengthen you and help you; I will uphold you with my righteous right hand."

When it comes to the outlook and vision of the world, sometimes as believers, we can get discouraged by what we see but it is so very important for us to stay vigilant and continue to be persistent in prayer, keeping the faith and never giving up. I would like to end this chapter by honoring Senator John McCain, who passed away on August 25th 2018. I honor him, not just because he was a brave soldier who was captured, and endured great torture for the sake of his country, and not just because he was deemed a hero to many. All of those things are true, and even though I did not always agree with his ideology, Senator McCain will always hold a special place in my heart and the hearts of many Americans from all walks of life because of the stand that he took against his party on July 28th 2017. He will always be remembered not just for his bravery during the Vietnam War and his time in captivity. He will always be remembered by millions of Americans as not only a war hero but also the hero who saved healthcare the image of the thumbs down will forever be engraved in our minds. I know he was making a statement to his party regarding the need for bipartisanism but I don't believe that even Senator McCain knew the enormity of his vote in the lives of those people such as me and others that may have a pre-existing condition. I would like to use this opportunity to show my gratitude to a great hero who will be missed. I would also like to take this time to thank former President Obama and all of the other Congressmen and Senators who supported and work so hard to fight for the average American to have the chance, some for the first time to have healthcare and for others like me to rest a little bit easier knowing I have protections under the law and my children will be able to be covered until twenty-six. As a nation, we should give credit where credit is due. We are more than capable of criticizing the leadership of this country so maybe we can take the time to be thankful when they do something right. I believe President Obama's legacy will stand, and history will judge him fairly, regardless of what anyone says or does because he made a conscious effort to show compassion towards the people with most of his policies and that means a lot.

I just did not think that politics could get any worse or could be any more divisive than the 2016 election but I was wrong. It was the day that the world witnessed the testimony of a professor by the name of Christine Blasey Ford, who put everything on the line, and boldly went before the Senate of the United States made up mostly of men, to tell her truth—of being held down and sexual assaulted at the age of fifteen. The alleged perpetrator is now a federal judge who has been nominated to the highest court of the land. A man with a lot of powerful supporters, and most importantly, he is known to have an impeccable reputation so when his accuser testified in front of the Senate and the world, it was riveting. She came across as authentic and very credible.

Any human being with an ounce of compassion could empathize and feel her pain as she spoke her truth. After the testimony of the accuser, the accused was up next to defend himself and tell his side of the story. His opening statement started off with a lot of passion and authenticity but somewhere around the middle of his opening statement, something changed. He became more aggressive in his delivery. He started to accuse the Democratic Senators of conspiring against him, and yes, he even dove headfirst into politics. I was astonished when he interjected the Clintons into his speech. The entire atmosphere changed and seemed to go dark from all of the rage, and it only got worse when he started to interact with the Democratic Senators. His demeanor appeared to me to go beyond anger—it was almost borderline belligerent. It was shocking and disappointing to see a potential Supreme Court justice act in such a manner, no matter what the circumstance. He seemed to evade every question that the Democratic Senators asked that seemed relevant, while the Republican Senators just made speeches apologizing to the judge, and making political statements about the process, making accusations and ridiculing the other side. What a sad day in America! It was so sad to see the disrespectful manner in which Christine Blasey Ford was treated, after the very powerful testimony she delivered. It was so disheartening to see how this process was managed, and how some Senators seemed so cold towards the alleged victim. Whether you believe the accuser or not, having respect for her truth is so important.

Our political system is more toxic than ever before on both sides. We, the people, just want our leaders to work together and realize it is not about having the most power and political capital. It is about serving the people. I pray someday they will get it or maybe it will be the next generation that will turn Washington around. My belief is that the court has been a political institution for some time now but the only difference today is that we are close to having a justice seated on the highest court in the land that seems to be very biased. This leads me to believe that he will not be able to be fair and impartial in making life-changing decisions. I pray to God that I am wrong. The Supreme court has become more political over the years to the point that maybe the justices should be elected or have term limits instead of being nominated for life by a sitting President and confirmed by Congress. This process is causing more division in the country instead of bringing us together. I thought the purpose of the confirmation process instead of election of Supreme Court Justices was to prevent political bias and to give the justices freedom to follow the constitution and the law without being influenced by either party. But apparently, this is mired in hypocrisy.

The Supreme Court appears to be turning into another broken institution that many Americans are losing faith in. I would suggest that there should be an independent justice on the court at all times to make sure the decisions are not politically motivated, and to my evangelical sisters and brothers as Christians, the Word of God teaches us to be vigilant, (ever awake and alert, sleeplessly watchful) so we will not be fooled by the enemy. That is why, it is so important that we seek the face of God even when it comes to supporting or standing by a person who has conservative values. We have to be so careful that we do not confuse being conservative with being a child of the King holy and set apart having a relationship with Jesus Christ. The meaning of holy is, "saintly; godly; pious; devout a holy life"; "entitled to worship or veneration as or as if sacred: a holy relic"; "having a spiritually pure quality: a holy love." *1 Peter 5:8*: "Be sober, be vigilant; because your adversary the devil, as a roaring lion, walked about, seeking whom he may devour:' I am praying that every professed Christian will continue to pray for wisdom and direction about everything that is going on in the country today. We have to go back to the source, that Hope of Glory that lives within, so we can draw from that source the insight needed to help us in making the right choices. Just think about this for a minute with everything we know about God from his word through his presence in worship and through our experiences. Would a just, loving, righteous, infinite, holy, supreme, compassionate and faithful God be pleased with his people supporting the chaos, division, ugliness, lies and hypocrisy that is being let loose by our leaders in Washington? I believe after all we know about the character of God, the answer would be no.

1 John 1: 5-7 says, "This is the message (of God's promised revelation) which we have heard from Him and now announce to you, that God is Light (He is holy, His message is truthful, He is perfect in righteousness), and in Him there is no darkness at all (no sin, no imperfection). If we say that we have fellowship with Him and yet walk in the darkness (of sin), we lie and do not practice the truth, but if we (really) walk in the light (that is, live each and every day in conformity with the precepts of God), as He Himself is in the light, we have (true, unbroken) fellowship with one another."

October 2nd 2018, was another sad day in this country. On this day, the leader of the free world went to the state of Mississippi in front of a huge crowd of his followers to mock and make fun of the women that testified in front of the nation and professed that a Supreme court nominee attempted to sexual assault her when she was a teenager, whether or not you believe the accused or the accuser we all need to be respectful and portray some human decency. The most disappointing part of that rally for me was not the men and women I saw in the crowd, laughing and cheering on the President of the United States degrading and insulting a possible sexual assault survivor. But what really gave me pause was the little boy that you could see in plain sight taking in all the ugliness, being groomed to believe it's ok to laugh and make fun of a woman that professed that she went through a horrible, painful ordeal in her youth. Is this really the message we want to send to our young people? It is already difficulty for women to come forth if they have been sexually assaulted—this will make it that much more difficult for them to tell their truths, and so, they will suffer in silence. They may develop problems later in life, relationship issues, alcoholism, drug abuse, promiscuity and mental disorders, if they do not receive the help that they need. I just hope and pray they have the courage to tell someone at the time of the incident because when years and years go by, memories start to fade, and details may become blurred, as far as critical evidence needed to get justice is concerned.

I know many people have asked why it takes some accuser so long to come forward and report incidents of sexual assault, abuse or molestation? Here's my take on the issue, first of all we have to consider the age of the victim at the time of the alleged assault, secondly, we must consider the generation in which the incident happened. Oftentimes in past generations, people thought differently. Males and females were viewed a lot differently. Some people had the mentality that boys will be boys. A lot of victims probably blamed themselves, and may have even felt some amount of shame. Each and every case should be reviewed on an individual basis. All the facts must be gathered and processed fairly in order for justice to be served. This will benefit the accuser and the accused. It disturbs me to see people smeared in the media and tried and convicted in the public and on social media instead of a court of law. We are walking onto dangerous grounds when we do not allow both parties to be heard before we make our judgments.

I believe we are all at risk of our democracy being lost, when an individual can have an accusation come out against them in the media, and it is deemed to be a fact on social media before any factual evidence or statements are presented. The accused may very well in fewer than forty-eight hours have their entire life ruined, whether they are guilty or not. So, we have to be so very careful that we do not prosecute people in the media on either side without having all the facts. And this is coming from a woman that has dealt with multiple traumas in my past.

I am about to do something at this moment that I did not think I would ever have the strength or courage to do, but I have learned overtime that God is my strength. *2 Corinthians 12:10*: "So I am well pleased with weaknesses, with insults, with distresses, with persecution, and with difficulties, for the sake of Christ; for when I am weak (in human strength), then I am strong (truly able, powerful, truly drawing from God's strength).

I believe he is leading me to speak my truth in this book to help others, and I will not be ashamed and intimidated by what people may think or say about me. As long as I have God on my side, no weapon formed against me shall prosper and anyone that speaks against me in judgment while speaking my truth will be condemned. *Isaiah 54:17* says, "No weapon that is formed against thee shall prosper; and every tongue that shall rise against thee in judgment thou shalt condemn. This is the heritage of the servants of the Lord, and their righteousness is of me, saith the Lord." So if your righteousness is in him, this applies to you too.

I am a survivor not a victim of sexual abuse. Yes, me, it happened many years ago and was perpetrated by different individuals. I was around seven or eight when it happened the first time, and even now, almost thirty plus years later, I can remember major details of each encounter, the apartments and the rooms in the apartment. I remember the first time it happened, the room that I was in had a bike in it and a dresser with a mirror that was in front of the bed, so I could see my reflection in the mirror. I don't remember the exact date or time of the incident but I remember that it was summer because I remember I had worn shorts. The memories are still buried in my mind, and although I was so very young, I still remember.

So, going back to the prior incident, yes, I can say I think after both testimonies and the fact that it was reported that the accuser passed a polygraph test and reported the incident in counseling along with the fact that she testified under oath before Congress, it seems more likely than not in this particular case, that she was being truthful. Of course, each case should be judged on its merits. We cannot afford to group all allegations together. Some people may ask, if it happened, why did you wait so long before speaking about the incident? As a young child, I was confused as to what was happening. I felt that what was happening to me was wrong but I was so embarrassed and ashamed that I didn't want anyone to know—certainly not my mother because she was a Christian woman, and I did not want her to be ashamed of me. She went to her grave not knowing that her only daughter was sexually abused as a child, and to be honest, I really do not know how I feel about that. It took me twenty-two years to share what happened to me with my husband of twenty-four years because every time you tell your truth, you will have to relive the pain and shame. So for all you that asked why the survivor waited so long to come out and tell her truth, I say do not judge, especially if you have never been through it. Just be thankful that you were spared and pray for the ones that have suffered any kind of trauma. Once again, we have to encourage and make the environment conducive for victims to come forth immediately.

For those of you that are worried about your sons and husbands being falsely accused, well, welcome to the everyday life of black and brown people. We have to deal with that truth on a daily basis, and have been for generations. No one wants a loved one to be falsely accused under any circumstance, so, of course, all the facts should be assessed carefully and put into perspective. It makes me so sad to see the country so divided and so many of the people of God decide to turn a blind eye to what is obviously so wrong. What are we willing to risk in order to win? Are we willing to risk our souls? "For what shall it profit a man, if he shall gain the whole world, and lose his own soul?": *Mark 8:36*.

I have heard some historians discuss how history will judge our leaders and the new norms which we are living with, including a lack of integrity, decency, honor, compassion and a lot of hypocrisy. Many believe that history will judge this season in time harshly but history is not our primary concern. Our primary concern is for those who know to do right or stand for what is right and do not. *James 4:17* says, "So any person who knows what is right to do but does not do it, to him it is sin." I say there are no gray areas when it comes to doing the right thing. It's either black or white, so at this point, two years into this chaotic, divisive political climate, if you are a believer and your eyes are not yet wide open to the truth, all I know to do is to keep praying that God will touch the hearts and minds of those warring within for truth. Will you believe that that small, still voice on the inside that is so softly telling you not to be deceived? Or will you believe that loud voice that spews confusion, divisiveness, pride, hate and lies? It is so important that we tune out the loud noise and focus on that calm, nurturing voice, deep down within us, trying to lead us and guide us back onto that righteous path. Can't you hear him speaking to your heart in that loving tone, trying to lead you back on the right path? Or will you continue to listen to that loud voice that's trying so desperately to lead you down the path of darkness? I pray that every stronghold will be broken off of the life of every believer in the Name of Jesus. "For the weapons of our warfare are not carnal but mighty in God for pulling down strongholds, 5 casting down arguments and every high thing that exalts itself against the knowledge of God, bringing every thought into captivity to the obedience of Christ." (2 Corinthians 10:4-5) *Proverbs 29:12 AMP* says, "If a ruler pays attention to lies and encourages corruption, all his officials will become wicked. *KJV* says, "If a ruler hearken to lies, all his servants are wicked." *2 Thessalonians 2-8* says, "Let no man deceive you by any means: for that day shall not come, except there come a falling away first, and that man of sin be revealed, the son of perdition; Who opposeth and exalteth himself above all that is called God, or that is worshipped; so that he as God sitteth in the temple of God, shewing himself that he is God. Remember ye not, that, when I was yet with you, I told you these things? And now ye known what withholdeth that he might be revealed in his time. For the mystery of iniquity doth already work: only he who now letteth will let, until he be taken out of the way. And then shall that Wicked be revealed, whom the Lord shall consume with the spirit of his mouth, and shall destroy with the brightness of his coming:"

I believe we have to really focus and pray for the next generation to come together and be unified, as believers, we have to hold on to our faith no matter how dark the world seems to be. Because as long as the presence of God continues to dwell in us, there will always be light. "Lord, I thank you for using the spiritual discernment in my life to become an asset to my family. Also allow it to bring a contribution to the Kingdom. Let information and revelation come to the saints through impartation. Let resources come to the church through equipping. Let discernment be turned on in the lives of your people through activation. I declare that the people of God will not be ignorant of the devices of the enemy, and they will sharply detect the wiles of darkness, in Jesus' name, I pray." Prayers that Bring Change by Kimberly Daniels Pg.15.

I would like to leave you with one last Scripture. *2 Timothy 4: 3-4* says, "For the time will come when people will not tolerate sound doctrine and accurate instruction (that challenges them with God's truth); but wanting to have their ears tickled (with something pleasing), they will accumulate for themselves (many) teachers (one after another, chosen) to satisfy their own desires and to support the errors they hold, and will turn their ears away from the truth and will wander off into myths and man-made fictions (and will accept the unacceptable)."

CHAPTER 6

The uncovered truth, race relations in the church

I would ask every believer in the body of Christ to go deep down within, where your soul is in search of the truth. When I speak of truth, I am not referring to your truth as you know it. I speak of the truth that will set your whole being free. When we look at the soul, it is defined as, "the principle of life, feeling, thought, and action in humans, regarded as a distinct entity separate from the body, and commonly held to be separable in existence from the body; the spiritual part of humans as distinct from the physical part"; "the spiritual part of humans regarded in its moral aspect, or as believed to survive death and be subject to happiness or misery in a life to come arguing the immortality of the soul"; "the emotional part of human nature; the seat of the feelings or sentiments."

The soul is the deepest part of our being. Without the soul, the body is no more. It returns to the ground. Sometimes, as Christians, we often deal with situations related to race on a surface level but we must learn to navigate beyond the outward boundaries. When dealing with racial inequality and injustices and a whole history of racism that plagues our nation today, we must go deep into the soul where the deep-seated issues are rooted. The seed sometimes has been planted so deep down on the inside that it goes unrecognized. The Holy Spirit will begin to reveal the things that are buried in the depths of our soul but are we willing to receive the truth and allow the Spirit to detect and remove any foul seeds that may have been planted when you were a child, or through a bad experience? "For the word of God is quick, and powerful, and sharper than any two-edged sword, piercing even to the dividing asunder of soul and spirit, and of the joints and marrow, and is a discerner of the thoughts and intents of the heart." *Hebrews 4:12.*

America is on a collision course that began shortly after the election of the first African American President. If we are truly honest about the matter, the emergence of The Tea Party movement was one of the catalysts that opened the door for the chaos that we find our country in today. The Tea Party movement according to Wikipedia is, "an American fiscally conservative movement within the Republican Party. Members of the movement have called for a decrease of the national debt of the United States and federal budget deficit by reducing government spending, and for lower taxes."

I wonder what happened to that movement once President Obama's last term was over. They are nowhere to be found, and fiscal responsibility went right out the window, and now the country can return to massive amounts of spending. I hear that word again, yes, you know the one—hypocrisy. There are so many racial issues that are plaguing the country as well as the church that we have yet to deal with. Until we go beyond the surface of those issues and reach the truth and deal with the truth as a country and as the body of Christ, we will never completely heal and be unified.

There are steps that we must take as the church to reach the desired outcome. Number one: we have to really stand on one accord and seek the face of God to receive true revelation in search of the truth. Secondly, once he reveals the truth, we have to receive it and repent. Next, we have to ask God to reveal the source because without us knowing the source, there is a good chance those racial tendencies may resurface; and lastly, we have to pray and ask God to totally remove forever that corruptible seed that has been buried so deep down on the inside of us that we may not recognize that it exists. We have to tackle this generational, demonic device of racism that has once again reared its ugly head but this time, it's coming at us in full force—like a missile that has been launched towards the church. It has even grown in size like a tumor and it will consume everything that gets in its destructive path. We pray and we pray against it, but sometimes, it seems the more we pray, the more it grows. However, we cannot get discouraged and lose our position on the battle field. Just like soldiers on the battlefield need sound strategies before entering the battlefield, we must seek God and his Word to receive strategy before entering the battle. Make no mistake, we are in a war. It's what believers call 'spiritual warfare'. So the battle has to be won in the spiritual realm first. It would be of great value if all the spiritual leaders of all races in the country would come together and seek the face of God about race relations in this country and in the church to receive directions as a body to combat this evil.

We have to recognize that the church is divided, and it also has a problem with race relations. We have to deal with the elephant in the room head on. The church has to wake up and see what is really in front of it before it is too late. I have to tell you the truth as the Body of Christ we have failed miserably, sometimes, we think we have it altogether but the reality couldn't be further from the truth, especially when it comes to race in this country. We have to open our eyes and see the truth, as a body, we are walking around going about our daily lives ignoring the fact that the world is in chaos, and that the racial and political divide are growing and causing us to grow further apart from each other and the kingdom of God.

If you would open your spiritual eyes, and allow the Holy Spirit to take control of your sight, the scales will be removed and your vision will become clearer. But who really wants to know the truth? Sometimes, it is hard for us to see the bad things that are buried down deep inside—such as, the ugliness, the pride, superiority, selfishness, superficiality. These are just some things that are hidden deep down on the inside of us that God wants to totally uproot. But we have to be willing participants in order for him to do it.

Now let's begin to look at the hard truth, I want to share with you an interesting article that I read online titled, "Here's what many white Christians fail to understand about the NFL protests," by Carol Kuruvilla. In reading this article, I came away with some interesting perspectives on the NFL protests. For one, the writer noted that "Christians of color have a radically different way of thinking about God and country," and I believe that to be true, based on my own thoughts and feelings and other Christians of color that I have talked to about the NFL protests. It's not shocking that we would feel differently. Even though we are Christians, we are also people of color who have unfortunately experienced some racism ourselves or known someone close to us who has had some negative encounter with law enforcement. We all know that not all officers are the same, but unfortunately, one negative encounter with one rotten apple can be life-changing. This article really enlightened me about some facts that I didn't know, one being that Colin Kaepernick is a devout Christian whose faith turned him into an activist, and we know of the many sacrifices that come with being an activist and standing up for a life-changing cause its similar to standing in the gap for others. The article focused on an op-ed in the *New York Times* that was written by Eric Reid, a former teammate of Colin who decided to risk his career and took a knee in protest along with his teammate.

Reid reported that Christianity moved him to take a knee. He also quoted a very profound scripture in the Bible saying faith without action is dead, and that is so true. He talked about the protest being tied to faith, the Kind of righteous indignation that fueled the civil rights movement in the 1960s. The article also discussed how some Christians expressed their dismay, "claiming that kneeling during the anthem is an unpatriotic and ungrateful gesture." "This fissure in response to the NFL protests highlights key differences between white Christians and Christians of color. These groups tend to think differently about racial justice and what Christianity should look like when it's called to action. The divide between American Christians about the appropriateness of protest for black lives isn't new." The author also quoted a letter that Dr. Martin Luther King wrote from a Birmingham Jail, in which he wrote about his disappointment with "white moderate" Christian leaders and churches that claimed they agreed with King's goals, but not his method. These Christians advised black activists to wait for a "more convenient season" for equality to materialize." Dr. King wrote, "I have almost reached the regrettable conclusion that the Negro's great stumbling block in his stride toward freedom is not the White Citizen's Councilor or the

Ku Klux Klanner, but the white moderate, who is more devoted to 'order' than to justice."

Now fast forward fifty years later into the 21st century, nothing has changed as far as the divide between white Christians and Christians of color is concerned. Yes, they may say that racism and inequality are wrong but when you look at the statistics and the silence of some of our white Christian leaders, it speaks volumes. "A 2015 PRRI (Public Religion Research Institute) survey found that 65 percent of white Christians agreed that when Americans in general speak up and protest against unfair treatment by the government, it always makes the country better. Sixty-two percent of nonwhite Americans said the same. But change the race of the people protesting, and the response looks significantly different. Only 44 percent of white Christians agreed that when black Americans speak up and protest against unfair treatment by the government, it always makes the country better. About 63 percent of nonwhite Christians agreed."

The article also mentioned the fact that white Christians are also less likely than Christians of color to understand the discrimination that minorities face now. I can understand why they would not be able to relate to the discrimination that African Americans have to face daily. It seems logical to me because we know that if you have never experienced discrimination, then you can't relate to it. But as Christians, we should be able to have empathy and compassion for one another.

If we profess to be a part of the body of Christ and that Hope of Glory dwells within every believer, then we should be able to share in each other's pain, even if we cannot relate to the experience. Whether your church is filled with black Christians, white Christians or multiracial members, we are one body. Therefore, the Church should be leading the charge against institutional racism, voter suppression, legislation that supports oppression of people of color, racial inequality, police brutality and all injustices in this country. We cannot leave it to a broken government to fix these issues alone; as the church, we cannot just pray but we should be encouraging people not just with hope but also with opportunity. I do not care what race you are —if you are a Christian, you should be concerned about so many young black men being institutionalized for years when often time the punishment does not fit the crime. The Word teaches us that we should have that same love for one another regardless of race. *John 13:34-35* says, "A new commandment I give to you, that you love one another: just as I have loved you, you also are to love one another. By this, all people will know that you are disciples, if you have love for one another."

I can truly tell you out of all the articles I have read when doing my research, the statistics provided by the PRRI on protests was disheartening, especially the studies that have shown that, "white Evangelicals are less likely than other religious groups and the unaffiliated to say that black Americans experience significant discrimination. While 36 percent of white evangelical Protestants say there is a lot of discrimination against black Americans in the U.S. today, 86 percent of black Protestants say the same." White evangelical Protestants were particularly likely to say that police officers treat blacks the same as whites, and they are the only major religious group in which a majority fifty-seven percent say the police killings of black men in Ferguson, New York City, and Baltimore were isolated incidents compared to seventy percent of minority Protestants who say these police killings were part of a broader pattern. After reading those statistics, one might ask, are we living in different Americas? The answer would be 'yes', it goes back to your culture, our environment, each person's individual experience and sometimes, we see what we want to see because the truth may be inconceivable for us. I am going to speak directly to my white evangelical brothers and sisters who believe that all police officers treat people of color the same as whites and that people of color do not experience a lot of discrimination. I am here to tell you as a Christian and a person of color not to be fooled by the enemy—that old demon of racism and discrimination is still alive and more viscous than ever since the 2016 election. People of color in some form of fashion see and experience some form of racism every day, whether it comes in the form of a spoken word, a common gesture or maybe even a certain look when you enter a store. Let's talk about the racial profiling that happens to people of color on a daily basis, yes, even to my family.

Can you imagine your children and loved ones being mistreated or frowned on because of the color of their skin? I would like to take this time to share some of my truths with you. Let me start with an incident dealing with my mother who was a loving, kind woman of God. You can talk to anyone who knew her, and they would tell you she would help anyone who was in need. She did not have a lot of money or possessions but she was rich in love, compassion, faith and the things of God. She labored for the kingdom of God by going to the nursing homes and hospitals to pray and encourage the sick. She would get in her car and drive to different churches and food banks in the area to collect food and deliver it to the older seniors and others who could not get out. She labored for many years, even in the midst of her own struggles of dealing with diabetes, heart disease, and renal disease. Regardless of how she felt, she pushed on.

So you can imagine how horrified I was when this great woman of God called me up to tell me about an encounter, she had with a Virginia Beach police officer who stopped her for a routine traffic stop. She told me that when the officer said he pulled her over for speeding, she responded by telling him that she did not think that she went over the speed limit. My mother said he yelled at her and threatened to take her to jail like she was a common criminal. She was compliant and respectful, so you can imagine my concern when I found out that a loving mother, grandmother, could have been taken to jail or worse over a simple traffic stop. Now keep in mind this was over twenty years ago. I was angry that she was treated with such disrespect. I asked her why didn't she get his badge number and put in a complaint against him. She told me that she was giving it over to God and he would fight her battles. She was a true warrior of God who was intertwined in him—may God rest her soul. You can find out more about who she was and how the glory of God shined on her life in her book (*The Miracle Child*).

I didn't truly understand at the time what it meant to give your problems over to God and let him fight your battles because I did not have a relationship with Jesus Christ. But once I was enlightened by the truth and accepted Christ into my heart, I began to receive and experience the benefits of being a child of God. If you call on him to do so he will fight for you. *Exodus 14:14* says, "The Lord will fight for you while you (only need to) keep silent and remain calm." *Romans 12:19-21:* "Beloved, never avenge yourselves, but leave the way open for God's wrath (and His judicial righteousness); for it is written (in Scripture), "Vengeance is mine, I will repay," says the Lord. But if your enemy is hungry, feed him; if he is thirsty, give him a drink; for by doing this, you will heap burning coals on his head." Do not be overcome and conquered by evil, but overcome evil with good.

As Christians, the Word of God teaches us in *1 Thessalonians 5:17* that we should pray constantly and be persistent in prayer. If you are a person of color during this day and age, it would behoove you to take this Scripture to heart, as we face threats all around us in a nation that's more divided than ever. It is so critical that we keep our loved ones lifted in prayer, especially our sons and husbands. I must admit when my husband or children walk out the door, sometimes I may get an uneasy feeling, so I find myself saying a prayer over them asking God to go before them, keep them covered under the blood of Jesus, and keep a hedge of protection all around them. No matter where they go and who they come in contact with, I pray that God will protect them. Although they know what to do and what not to do, if they come in contact with the police, Prayer will give you peace— peace that only God can give, and a peace that surpasses all understanding. *Philippians 4:7* says, "And the peace of God, which surpasses all understanding, will guard your hearts and your minds in Christ Jesus." We need that peace that only God can give to us in order to survive.

If you are a Christian of color, you probably have experienced or know someone who has experience some type of racism on some level. My family and I have dealt with some form of racism throughout our lives. Sometimes it was presented in a subtle form and during other instances, it was overt. I would like to share with you another instance where this old, historic evil has impacted my life. Just imagine your eldest son coming to you after being profiled and pulled over by a police officer when driving home one night. He was not pulled over for a traffic violation or a busted taillight. He was pulled over because the officer claimed that he crossed the yellow line over into the other lane, and therefore he must have been driving under the influence. He was stopped, instructed to get out of the car and take the Standardized Field Sobriety test and a Breathalyzer, which he passed with flying colors because he had zero alcohol in his system. After being humiliated, the officer had the audacity to tell him that he wasn't convinced that he wasn't drinking and driving, but because he passed the Breathalyzer test, he let him go on his way.

I have to be honest with you, as a mother I was angry after learning the trauma that my child was put through, and the thought of what could have happened to him if he had not been educated on what to do and how to act if he was ever stopped by the police. I was very concerned but at the same time I was thankful to God because it could have gone another way. It is sad but very vital that all children of color, especially young black boys are educated on what to do and how to respond to law enforcement, even if they believe they haven't done anything wrong. They have to know that sometimes they are judged by a different standard and usually will not get the benefit of the doubt.

We have to be real about this fact. No matter how respectful we are, how articulate and educated we may be, there will always be ignorant people who will see us in a negative light based on the color of our skin. But the good thing is that we are a resilient people with a lot of faith. God put strength in our DNA. Going all the way back to slavery, he created us to be resilient because he knew what we would have to face as a people. We have to continue to be strong and determined, and not let people define who we are. I have dealt with many instances of racism on a much personal level. I have been called the 'N' word on more than one occasion. My husband and his brother were racially profiled just recently at a bowling alley that they bowl at every other weekend. This evil has reared its ugly head many times. Practically everyone in my immediate family, including my brother who is blind, has dealt with it. Recently there was an incident—he was trying to find his way back home after getting confused about the direction he should have been walking in. So, after hearing a car next to him as he stood on the curb, he asked the occupant of the vehicle if they could tell him the name of the street he was on because he had lost his direct

I would like to give you one last example about my truth, and this truth dealt with a situation that happened to my twenty-two-year-old daughter and two of her friends. They were on summer break and decided to go to the movies to see a scary movie, and towards the end of the movie, during one of the scenes, one of my daughter's friends was startled and screamed— because normally that's what some people do when watching scary films. Well, a white, middle age woman sitting three chairs down from them yelled at my daughter's friend to be quiet. The young lady, in response, pointed out that there were other seats in the theater if she felt she needed to move. So, of course, that response did not sit well with the other patron, who retorted, "You think you're a tough, little lady? You're going to get kicked out of here!" And so, she proceeded to leave the theater to complain and she returned, armed with the manager, a security guard and a police officer.

You would have thought they were a huge threat. So, based on one complaint from an aggressive, middle-aged, white woman, about one scream during a scary movie, they were humiliated and escorted out of the theater. As they were leaving the theater, other people in the theater were wondering what was happening and what they had done, because the only person they saw or heard being loud and aggressive was the woman who had complained. When my daughter was telling me the story, of course, she felt they were being treated that way because of the color of their skin. Once outside the theater, they tried to plead their case to no avail and the officer told them, if they did not leave, they would be trespassing. They all knew what that meant, so they immediately left the theater while the one person causing the big spectacle was allowed to stay and enjoy the rest of the movie. You can imagine how upset I was as a parent. But I was also grateful they remained respectful in the midst of what was so unfair and humiliating. As they exited the theater, they had other older black women in the theater telling them to keep their heads up. I was very upset and considered contacting the corporate office to write a formal complaint against the manager but somehow, I could hear my mom from twenty plus years ago saying, "I gave it to the Lord and he will fight my battle." So, I just prayed about it and was led to share their story.

I wanted to share a small portion of some of the discrimination over the years that has impacted my family. So, for all those individuals in the 2015 PRRI study that do not believe that black Americans experience significant discrimination, I have two words for you, "Wake Up!" As an African American Christian, I will continue to pray tirelessly for that hedge of protection over my family because for me it is necessary. The Word teaches us in *Colossians 4:2*: "Be persistent and devoted to prayer, being alert and focused in your prayer life with an attitude of thanksgiving."

I want to go back to the article that I discussed earlier in the chapter that dealt with the division on kneeling during the national anthem. I tried to approach this sensitive issue fairly and from both sides. In the article, Rev. Jacqueline Lewis, senior minister of New York City's Middle Collegiate Church, told *Huff Post* that, "she believes the flag is a symbol of the freedoms the country claims to uphold—freedom to " drive, work, and live while Black. Vote while Black. Raise children while Black. Safely." But America isn't there yet. "I think the deeper issue is that for African Americans in this nation, that flag and that national anthem are only as sacred as the willingness of those who sing and salute to stand up for the lives of all Americans, to stand against white supremacy—the white supremacy that built this land on the backs of enslaved Africans, after stealing it from first nation peoples," Lewis said. The Rev. Traci Blackmon, a United Church of Christ pastor deeply involved with racial justice ministries, told *Huff Post* that to her, "the flag and the national anthem are symbolic reminders of the ideals that America has not yet realized." As a result, she says, a football game is the "perfect place" for Kaepernick and others to protest. Valerie Cooper, Associate Professor of Religion and Black Church Studies at Duke Divinity School, said that "one of the ways that black churches think of Jesus is as the leader of a protest movement—someone who came to earth to proclaim good news to the poor and set the captive free." I thought Valerie Cooper made an interesting point when she said, "Protest is never convenient for the people being protested against. The real question is, when is it time for justice? If it is really justice we seek, it's always the right time."

The other side makes a completely different perspective. The article said Robert Jeffress, a Southern Baptist pastor who is one of President Trump's tops evangelical advisors, claimed that "the NFL players should be eternally grateful to God that they live in a country where they aren't 'shot in the head' for protesting." The only response I have to that is "Wow!" That could be misconstrued as a racist statement. If I had a chance to meet Pastor Jeffress, I would ask him to go back and take a good look at his words and how that statement may be looked upon as racist and hurtful. We all, including Pastor Jeffress, should be eternally grateful to God for all things. As Christians, the Word of God teaches us that our words matter and we have to be careful when we speak. After all, we are representatives of Christ. *Proverbs: 15-1* says, "A soft and gentle and thoughtful answer turns away wrath. But harsh and painful and careless words stir up anger." Attorney General Jeff Sessions, a staunch defender of religious liberty, said the players should make their protest in "any other place." "As a matter of propriety, of love of country, and decency, you should stand when the national anthem is played," Sessions said. The article also mentioned that even the Christians in the study that agreed the players' free speech should be protected didn't think protesting the anthem was the best way to seek justice. The article also reported on the fact that for some black Christians, the flag, the anthem, and other patriotic symbols are inextricably tied to America's racist past. And the Jesus of the Bible, with his message of liberation and radical inclusivity, is seen as someone who is intimately associated with struggle for justice.

I would like to take this time to give you my opinion regarding this issue, and I will start with telling you a personal situation that may give you some insight into how all the controversies going on in this country have some impact on our kids. Whether you see it or not, some are suffering in silence, some are acting out and some may just be confused about how the adults are behaving in this hostile, divisive environment. As Christians, we have to teach them to respect the rights of others, be kind to one another, to always try and be honest and tell the truth but when they are seeing the opposite behavior in the leadership and the adults in this country, it must be confusing to them. The personal story that I wanted to share with you is about my son, who at the time was almost thirteen years old. It was sometime after the 2016 election, and at the height of the NFL protest and young black men being killed. One day, I received an email from one of my son's teachers who told me that my son and one other young man sat during the Pledge of Allegiance. He said that he pulled the boys aside, and had a conversation about why he felt it was important for them to stand for the Pledge of Allegiance, and with him being a veteran who served his country, he explained to the boys why he felt not standing for the pledge was a sign of disrespect towards the military. He said my son did comply, and was respectful after he spoke to him, and the teacher asked if my husband and I could speak with him further about the situation. I really had to take the time to gather my thoughts before responding to his email because I wanted to speak our truth without offending someone who served this country.

I started off by saying that I did understand his perspective on the matter, and how not standing for the pledge could be seen by some as a form of disrespect against the military. I assured him that this was not the case. In fact, we could relate because my father served in the United States Navy and my uncle the great and honorable William A Cason served on the battlefield in the Vietnam war—yes, on the battlefield where the bodies of U.S. soldiers were falling all around him. So as a people, we know all about sacrifice. I also asked him to try to understand where my thirteen-year-old son was coming from, seeing on the news every time he turned around that a young black male had been killed by someone in authority. Add to this, all the division and bad feelings caused by the 2016 election. I asked his teacher to take all this into consideration before making any judgments.

I ended my email by letting him know that my husband and I would talk to our son to let him know that we do want him to continue to follow the rules and be respectful to everyone, and that's exactly what we did. We also let our son know that we understood his concerns and fears about all the turmoil going on in this country and that he had every reason to feel the way he felt; but we have to continue to pray for this country. We let him know that we were proud of him for taking a stand for what he believed in but at the same time we wanted him to be compliant and stay focused on his education while in school. He is a bright young man, filled with so much compassion and promise, so we let him know that right now, there was a better way for him to engage in the fight for justice and equality, and it doesn't include him sitting down but it includes him standing up, working hard to get good grades, continue to be respectful to all people and focus on getting a good education. Because education is the key for young black men.

Once again, for all you who do not know that the last four years have had a definite impact on our children, I suggest you take a second look. *Proverbs 22:6* says, "Train up a child in the way he should go, and when he is old, he will not depart from it." We can learn from our kids and the way that they see the world and how they simply see what is right Versus wrong, good Versus evil. With them, there's no gray area, it's only black and white. *Matthew 18:2-5:* "He called a little child and sent him before them, and said, 'I assure you and most solemnly say to you, unless you repent (that is, change your inner self-your old way of thinking, live changed lives) and become like children (trusting, humble, and forgiving), you will never enter the kingdom of heaven. Therefore, whoever humbles himself like this child is greatest in the kingdom of heaven. Whoever receives and welcomes one child like this in my name receives me'."

I know that the NFL protests have been a very sensitive issue for all Americans, regardless of what side of the debate you may agree with. The protests started with one man kneeling in front of millions of people during the National Anthem. I do not believe he intended to show any type of disrespect to our brave men and women of the military who have put their lives on the line to protect our democracy. His apparent intent was to protest against the injustice and the killings of unarmed young black men by cops. Now does that mean he is saying that all officers are bad or racist? I would say absolutely not. I commend officers for putting their lives on the line every day. Both sides have to face the facts. There are a lot of evil people in our world today just waiting to do harm to others, so where would we be today without those officers who take that oath to protect and serve all people, no matter what the color of their skin may be? Those of you who are against the protest must face the fact that there are racist officers on the force who do treat and enforce the law differently when it comes to people of color. Maybe instead of denying that the problem exists, let's focus on the root of the problem and fixing it. I believe that the players who are kneeling mean no disrespect to the flag or the country—the kneeling was a way for them to be seen and heard. I know very well what the flag symbolizes and the honor that is attached to it, especially when you witness that honor up close and personal. I have had the chance, unfortunately, to witness this honor on two occasions. At my uncle's funeral—he was a veteran who served for many years, and one of my good friend's husband. He too served his country for many years. Both men were honorable men who deserved the respect of their country and that United States flag being draped over their caskets, folded up so perfectly and handed to their wives with such grace. It is a proud but heart wrenching experience. We can agree to disagree with each other in love. We should be more understanding and take the time to actually listen to each other's perspective without judgment. As Christians, we have to do all things in love. We should be the examples for the world and represent Christ.

With that being said, I would like to take this time to discuss another article that I read from the *New York Times* website, written by Mark Oppenheimer. 'Some Evangelicals struggle with Black Lives Matter movement.' Yes, this was the title of the commentary. The writer talked about how many Christian groups support and have become active with the Black Lives Matter movement. The article quoted some Christian groups that have given support to the movement but according to the writer these groups are more liberal thinking. The article also dealt with the fact that conservative evangelical groups, "would all agree that black lives, like other lives, matter. But evangelicals who support Republican candidates are uncomfortable with the movement because of its embrace of liberal politics, associated with Democrats." As Christians, the Word of God teaches us that we are not to be conformed to this world. 'Conformed' means, "to act in accord with the prevailing standards, attitudes, practices, etc., of society or group: One has to conform in order to succeed in this company. To be or become similar in form, nature or character." Is our political association more important than our association with Christ and walking upright before him? The Black Lives Matter movement is not a liberal cause—it's a human cause, and if you are a Christian, and that is hard for you to see, then I pray that you would seek the face of God about the movement, and he will lead you and guide you to the truth. "Do not be conformed to this world, but be transformed by the renewal of your mind, that by testing you may discern what is the will of God, what is good and acceptable and perfect." *Romans 12:2.*

As Christians, we all know that all lives matter but I believe it is important to point out that unfortunately, we live in a society that does not always recognize that fact. Yes, even in the church today, we have people who are totally detached from that reality. We know the love that Jesus shared for all men when he walked the earth many years ago, and today by his spirit and word. I do not believe he factors in our race with the equivalence of how important our lives, and most importantly, our souls are to him. So when the response to 'Black Lives Matter' is 'All Lives Matter', I would say yes, we are just trying to get you to see that exact point.

Jesus has given us the command to love, out of all the commands, this seems to be the most important one, and without that love for one another, we could not survive. "And this commandment we have from him: whoever loves God must also love his brother." *1 John 4:21*: Let's discuss another form of racism at the highest level—a systematic well-planned attempt to disenfranchise people of color from voting and having a say in democracy. The scheme is bolder and more rampant now, especially since the election of the first African American President. After the 2010 election, lawmakers from mostly Southern states introduced legislation making it harder to vote, introducing new laws that range from strict ID requirements to early voting cutbacks to registration limits. Twenty-five states have put in place new limits since that time. The individuals who are participating in this theft of democracy are our leaders, and it is overwhelmingly coming from Southern and Midwestern parts of the country. A prime example is the 2018 Governor's race in Georgia which from the very beginning was mired in conflict, considering the person in charge of overseeing the election was actually in the race—a person who was on tape boldly admitting that the best way to win was to have fewer people voting, purging people off of the rolls without their knowledge, passing new, stricter voter ID requirements that mostly affects the poor, elderly and people of color, closing down polling sites in certain neighborhoods to produce longer lines and wait times to discourage people from casting their votes, changing voters' polling sites, moving them further away from their homes, and the most notorious of them all—the exact match law. A law that requires that citizens' names on their government-issued IDs must precisely match their names as listed on the voter rolls, so, if a hyphen is missing or the individual writes down their initials instead of their middle name, or just having a discrepancy in one letter in a voter's name, the person cannot vote. So, this law has done exactly what it was meant to do, and that was to stop valid voters from casting their votes.

For all those good people who say that we need strict voter laws to prevent the voter fraud that has been going on, you can breathe a sigh of relief. Know that just about every study that has been done found very low incident rates of fraud, and most of those could be traced back to human error. The most disheartening thing about this injustice is that the highest court in the land, whose very job is to protect and uphold the constitution for the people, had a direct hand in this injustice—by cancelling key parts of the voting rights act of 1965 with a five-to- four vote decision in 2013, allowing nine states mostly out of the South to change election laws without prior federal approval.

In my view, it was if they gave those states with a history of discrimination, a loaded gun to discriminate. The court was divided along ideological lines, and the basis for the argument was whether racial minorities continued to face barriers to voting in states with a history of discrimination, and for five out of four of the justices, the answer was 'no'—so just like that they opened the flood gates for this country to go backwards. Chief justice John Roberts in his response for the majority went as far to say, "Our country has changed. While any racial discrimination in voting is too much, Congress must ensure that the legislation it passes to remedy that problem speaks to current conditions." We all hope and pray the leaders of every state will do the right thing, but unfortunately, history teaches us a different lesson.

Another prime example is congresswoman from the state of Mississippi who won a place in the US Senate even after she made a comment joking about a public hanging. Of all the things to joke about in the deep South, hanging should be off limits in any situation. But after everything was said and done, she won the Senate race by eight points—after all, the South is the South. The saddest thing about this win is that most of the white evangelical Christians stayed true to their conservative roots. I don't care what the color of your skin may be, if you are a believer, any type of discrimination should concern you, not just because it is wrong but because of the love of Christ in your heart that gives you that compassion for others. *Psalm 89:14* says, "Righteousness and justice are the foundation of your throne; Loving, kindness and truth go before you."

There is one last controversial topic in this chapter that I would like to confront, and that would be the use and the meaning behind the Confederate flag. I really want to take the time to understand the perspective of others about why it is necessary to have the Confederate flag displayed in public buildings, schools, and yes, even churches or anywhere in any circumstance. The Confederate flag represented the Confederate States of America, the group of Southern slave-holding states that seceded from the Union in 1861, before dissolving at the end of the Civil War four years later. It was the subject of a controversial debate in 2000 that ended with its removal from the top of the South Carolina statehouse dome. Some believe the flag is a symbol of Southern resistance in respect to ending slavery, and there also some Christians in the South that continues to support the flag, according to a CNN article in 2015, written after the Charleston Church shooting that stated, "the flag also has its share of Christian sympathizers, particularly in the South, in part because its design incorporates St. Andrew's Cross. Some Christians believe the symbol represents the diagonal cross on which Andrew, one of Jesus's disciples, was crucified. Russell Moore, president of the Ethics and Religious liberty Commission of the Southern Baptist Convention, wrote a blog that went viral after the shootings in a Charleston church in 2015." In his blog, he wrote about the need, for Christians with Southern conservative sympathies to let go of their allegiance to the flag.

I agree with his blog because that symbol does represent a lot of pain and suffering for an entire race of people, and it is a constant reminder of this darkness in America's history. This flag is tied to many horrible things such as slavery, separation, racism, brutality and murder by hanging, (public lynching). So why is it still ok for this flag to continue to hang in public places up and down the South? The number one reason we hear from the Southerners who continue to support the Confederate flag being hung in and outside of public buildings along with the Confederate statues of generals that rebelled and broke the law is because they could not or would not let go of their need for power and domination over a people, they consider to be less than human. Some believe that this is their heritage and getting rid of the symbols would be like erasing their history.

Dictionary.com defines heritage as "something that is handed down from the past, as a tradition: a national heritage of honor, pride, and courage." I would like to know where is the honor in fighting to continue to enslave and brutalize an entire race of people for financial gain? When I was a child growing up in the state of Virginia, at some point when I was in elementary school, we would take a field trip to Williamsburg, Virginia, to see all the historic properties such as the Jamestown Settlement, and Colonial National Historical Park. We got to see all the historic monuments such as Yorktown Battlefield. My point is that there is a place for all those Confederate statues and flags to be stored and put on display for all who wish to see them. As Christians, no matter what race you may belong to, if someone or something is causing your brother and or sister in Christ pain, no matter what the color of their skin may be, it should concern you also, since after all, we are a part of the same body of Christ. When one part of the body is hurting in some way, it's going to impact the rest of the parts because they all are connected.

I would like to end this chapter with a word I received from Kenneth Copeland Ministries, '7 ways to destroy the spirit of racism". The message was about how the root of racism is the spirit of division, and how that giving place to this spirit in the Church, our country and families is dangerous. He referenced *Matthew 12:25 (KJV)* which says, "Every kingdom divided against itself is brought to desolation, and every city or house divided against itself shall not stand." He also made a good point, that we cannot afford to let the spirit operate unhindered, "and it starts with each of us making a quality decision to reject the spirit of division." I second that motion, so people of God, let's get delivered from this evil before it is too late. As I said in one of the chapters before, I have been a small business owner for more ten years. As a matter of fact, it's been since 2008—so this April, it will be twelve years. I have a partner, and we provide personal care services to the elderly and the disabled.

Anything dealing with healthcare is never easy but we do the best that we can, considering what we have had to deal with over the past twelve years. We have dealt with low reimbursement rates for many years, and that makes it very hard to take care of all of the responsibilities of the business and continue to give the very loyal employees the pay they deserve. Although we have only received three increases in over twelve years, we try very hard to give our employees raises even when the business does not receive one. We know in our hearts that God will make the provision for the vision. The last three years have been one of the most difficult times of our process but by the grace of God, we are still here serving our community. My partner and I have often discussed reasons why the reimbursement rate still remains so low in 2020. When you look at the demographics in our state, personal care agencies are owned and run by many African Americans, and ninety- five percent of the workers in our industry are black. So, it makes us wonder if race is the reason why the reimbursement rates have remained so low over the past twelve years. The economy has been doing well for some time until the recent pandemic, so the lack of funding is unlikely. The only likely conclusion is that we may be dealing with a form of systematic racism.

I hope and pray that we are wrong but it is more likely than not that this may be the case. There have been many times when we have gone with little or no pay, in order to pay our employees. We have contemplated giving up so many times but, in those times, God would always give us a word and some form of hope, strengthening us to continue. We have learned that the journey and the assignment are not always easy but God will equip his people to complete every assignment, no matter how hard it maybe. *1 Samuel 16:7* says, "But the Lord said to Samuel, "Do not look at his appearance or at the height of his stature, because I have rejected him. For the Lord sees not as man sees; for man looks at the outward appearance, but the Lord looks at the heart."

CHAPTER 7

Love trumps hate

According to Dictionary.com, 'love' means, "affectionate concern for the well-being of others: the love of one's neighbor"; "the benevolent affection of God for His creatures, or the reverent affection due from them to God." In contrast, it says 'hate' means, "to dislike intensely or passionately, feel extreme aversion for or extreme hostility toward; detest: to hate the enemy, to feel intense dislike, or extreme aversion or hostility."

We all know that love and hate are two of the strongest emotions that a person can ever experience. But of course, we know one emotion is used for good and the other is used for bad. When it comes to our heavenly Father, his love for us runs so deep that in this lifetime we will never understand the totality of his love. But as Christians, we have to show love towards one another. It is so much easier to love than to hate. I would imagine that it takes much more energy to hate one another Versus loving one another, so please stop wasting your energy on hate.

I would like to take this time to touch on a very sensitive subject—the increase in hate crimes in the United States. According to FBI, the amount of hate crimes reported to the FBI in 2017 compared to 2016 increased by about 17 percent. The report was released in the FBI's annual 'Hate Crime Statistics' the report—a compilation of bias-motivated incidents submitted to the FBI by 16,149 law enforcement agencies. The statistics showed that, "59.6% of victims were targeted because of the offender's race/ethnicity/ancestry bias; 15.8% were targeted because of sexual-orientation bias; 1.6% were targeted because of gender identity bias; and 0.6% were targeted because of gender bias. Sixty-nine multiple bias hate crime incidents were also reported."

One thousand six hundred seventy-nine religious bias crimes were reported in 2017, and 58.1% were anti-Jewish and 18.6% were anti-Muslim. We are now at the end of 2018, and the country has sustained some real tragedies in the last four years or so, starting with the Charleston church shooting in June 2015, when a young white 21-year-old young man filled with ignorance and hate targeted and killed nine African-Americans, including the pastor during a prayer service in a church. The young man apparently wanted to start a race war. June 17, 2015, was another sad and painful day in American history.

We know there is an enemy that roams throughout the earth influencing and encouraging the fragile minds of people so full of hate and ignorance that it will eventually lead them a down a dangerous path. We can learn a lot from the families of the victims that gave their impact statement during the shooter's arraignment and chose to forgive the lost and misguided individual who so easily took the lives of their loved ones in a place that is sacred. Another incident of hate where a twenty-one-year-old filled with a lot of hate and ignorance, in August of 2017, deliberately drove his car into a crowd of people protesting a white nationalist rally, killing a thirty-two-year-old young lady and injury others in the crowd. It was another sad day in America's history, with that spirit of hate rearing its ugly head once again through ignorance. In times like these, we expect our leaders to come together and bring everyone together but unfortunately in one of those tragedies that did not occur.

I do not feel the need to rehash the response from our leader. We are painfully aware of the response. In light of the FBI statistics report that showed that anti-Semitic hate crimes spiked 37 percent in 2017. And if that wasn't bad enough, 2018 unleashed more hate upon the land, including a mass shooting in a Pittsburg synagogue in October 2018—a tragic event for the entire country. To add insult to the injury, this tragic event happened during a time when the country is more divided than ever.

The leaders, political pundits, TV networks of this country must be so careful about what they say and how they say it. The media also has a huge responsibility when it comes to the atmosphere of the country by way of what topics they choose to report on and the tone in which the news is reported. All networks need to be held accountable for misleading their viewers and striking a tone that causes more harm than good. At some point, it can become unhealthy for the country to be consumed by bad news repeated over and over again. It will eventually become overwhelming for the average person who does not have mental challenges. But for the individuals who are already mentally unstable and have unrealistic thoughts, tainted views filled with hate may be a recipe for tragedy. Look at the attack on a church in 2015, a night club shooting in 2016, a synagogue in 2018, and two innocent people gunned down and killed at a Kroger store in Kentucky one day after the shooting at the synagogue. All of those murders have one thing in common: HATE.

I would like to tell you about a documentary that I saw a couple of months ago that dealt with a hate crime in Jackson Mississippi that was so disturbing that it sent shock waves through an already divided community. The murder of forty-seven-year-old James Craig Anderson on June 26, 2011 perpetrated by Deryl Dedmon, who was eighteen years old at the time. The victim was an African American male—father, son, friend, brother—and according to the investigation the victim had apparently lost his keys, and was trying to get into his vehicle, when a group of white teenagers pulled up in a jeep into the parking lot the victim was in, and then proceeded to call another group of friends to let them know they had found a good target to perpetrate this horrible crime on. Apparently, this group of white teens had plotted, planned and perpetrated acts of violence against other people of color before they got to Mr. Anderson. According to the documentary, the district Attorney report per witness citing, once this group of white teens got to the victim in the parking lot, they "repeatedly beat him and robbed him."

One witness reported that one of the perpetrators yelled, "white power" after the beating. While one of the group of teens drove away, the second group of teens were in the truck with the perpetrator that purposely drove his pickup truck over Mr. Anderson, "who was staggering along the edge of the lot." This portion of the attack was apparently caught on video. It was later determined that the final attack of running the victim over with the truck is what caused Mr. Anderson's death a few days later. But the most disturbing part of this hate crime is the report that, this teenage boy later bragged about beating and running the victim over, saying "I ran that nigger over," to his accomplices in the jeep. Law enforcement officials reported that the perpetrator repeated the same statement, including the racial slur in other conversations. The killer and his accomplices were charged and convicted with one of the charges being a hate crime.

Initially, it was hard for me to see anything good that came out of this tragedy but now there are two good things in this horrible tragedy that we may be able to take comfort in. One major thing was the level of forgiveness that the victim's family showed towards the person that brutally murdered their love one. The person that actually caused the death of Mr. Anderson was indicted on charges of capital murder and a hate crime, and the other ten people that were involved and participated in some form or fashion in the crime were indicted on various charges. The thing that really stood out to me is that in the midst of all the hate, forgiveness and love were on display when the victim's sister wrote a letter on behalf of the Anderson family to the District Attorney in charge of the case. She asked for mercy on behalf of the ones responsible for the death of their love one and pleaded that the perpetrator be spared the death penalty because of their Christian values. The love of Christ was truly on display in the midst of what seemed so horrible. His light can never be extinguished—even in our darkest hour, the light of his love will always break through. So that is why we know that love trumps hate and that love will always win over hate, and as Christians, we do not have to live our lives in search of love when we have the love of Christ deep down on the inside.

There may be times in life when we may have to go way down deep inside to pull from the love, he shares within us on a daily basis in order to forgive people in certain situations such as the brutal murder of a loved one. But if we choose not to forgive and let bitterness seep in, that bitterness can turn into hate, and that hate will ultimately consume, and destroy everything that it comes in contact with. I would like to end this chapter by giving you the wisdom from the proverbs of Solomon: "Hatred stirs up strife, but love covers and overwhelms all transgressions (forgiving and overlooking another's faults)".

Proverbs: 10 and 12. (1st John 3:15-16) says, "Everyone who hates (works against) his brother (in Christ) is (at heart) a murderer (by God's standards); and you know that no murderer has eternal life abiding in him. By this we know (and have come to understand the depth and essence of His precious) love: that He (willingly) laid down His life for us (because He loved us). And we ought to lay down our lives for the believers." The Word is clear—if we are brothers and sisters in Christ, and if an offense comes against one of us, it comes against all of us, no matter what the color of our skin may be. The way that we look at the body as a whole, we have to look at one another in the same way. If one part of my body is hurting, I have to do my best to take care of and support that part of my body. As Christians, we must begin to not only see the truth but live the truth. God, I pray you will continue to open the hearts and minds of your people to receive and act on the truth in Jesus' name.

CHAPTER 8

The church, humanity and nationalism

According to Dictionary.com, the definition of 'humanity' is, "the quality or condition of being human, human nature"; "the quality of being humane; kindness; benevolence." Now let's take a look at the meaning of 'nationalism'. According to Dictionary.com, 'nationalism' means, "devotion and loyalty to one's own country; patriotism"; "the desire for national advancement or political independence"; "the policy or doctrine of asserting the interest of one's own nation viewed as separate from the interest of other nations or the common interests of all nations."

On the surface, this doesn't sound so bad—that is, putting the interest of your own first, and if we have the President of the United States declaring that he is a nationalist, then how can it be considered wrong or harmful. Of course, the first thing we need to do is search the Scripture to find exactly what the Word tells us about nationalism. What Jesus said about this issue... What instructions did Jesus give to us as the body of Christ to follow?

I did a little research and came across an interesting article named "Reclaiming Jesus," and the author's opening statement talked about the fact that they believed, "the soul of the nation and the integrity of faith are now at stake." And that, "it is time to be followers of Jesus before anything else—nationality, political party, race, ethnicity, gender, geography—our identity in Christ precedes every other identity." Another statement that I found to be spot-on was, "When politics undermines our theology, we must examine the politics. The church's role is to change the world through the life and love of Jesus Christ." So how do we fulfill that role if we believe in isolating ourselves and taking care of our own, staying in our own little communities with no concern for other nations? I would ask all those who may believe that nationalism causes no harm or being considered a nationalist is in step with Christianity. I would just ask you to marinate on what Christianity means and what is attached to that word, yes, I am referring to the Christ part. Just ask yourself if Jesus would ever consider being a nationalist or being ok with his children who may be leaning towards supporting or currently identify with the ideology of nationalism. If the Word teaches us that God gives a command to love one another, does that not include people all over the world? *1 Thessalonians 4:9* says, "Now concerning brotherly love you have no need for anyone to write to you, for you yourselves have been taught by God to love one another." *1 Corinthians 10:24* says, "Let no one seek his own good, but the good of his neighbor."

So, if the Word teaches us how crucial it is for us to follow the command of love, then what do Christianity and nationalism have in common? I read an article written by Eugene Scott from the *Washington Post* that reported on some astonishing polls that were conducted. One poll found, "More than half of white evangelicals say America's declining white population is a negative thing." "More than half 52 percent-of white evangelical Protestants say a majority of the U.S. population being nonwhite will be a negative development," according to the Public Religion Research Institute and the Atlantic. The sad part about that poll was that it wasn't shocking that over half of those people in the poll felt that way, but what was shocking to me is they admitted it when asked.

Another interesting part of the article, was the quote from an author by the name of Jemar Tisby, who is the author of *'The Color of Compromise'* which stated, "the truth about the American Church's complicity in racism, "told the fix that many white evangelicals tend to conflate Christianity with nationalism." It did make me wonder how it was possible to have that many Christians identify with white nationalists. I am not that naïve to believe that everyone that identifies with or may say they are Christians, are necessarily connected to that power source that brings truth and Revelation, yes, I am referring to that hope of Glory and the Spirit of God that can live on the inside of every believer. If you are a Christian that has a relationship with that source of love; it seems to me that all those that responded to that poll with a yes, may have to revisit their relationship with the source that teaches us to esteem others higher than ourselves. As Christians, should we be in support of our government building a wall to stop immigrants from entering the country? Should we be concerned as Christians, about the way human beings mostly running from a dangerous situation and trying to obtain a better life are being treated when they enter the country? Should we be ok with innocent children being separated from their parents, being held in cages and or sleeping on the floor? Could you imagine as a parent, no matter what race you may be, your child being treated in that manner? The statistics on how some Christians feel about immigration even gets worse, in a *Vox* article that depicted some shocking numbers, a Pew Research Center poll completed in May of 2018 found, "sixty-eight percent of white evangelicals say that America has no responsibility to house refugees, a full 25 points over the national average. Just twenty-five percent of those polled said, they think Americans should house refugees, white mainline Protestants, black Protestants, and Catholics all express support for refugees by between forty-three and sixty -five points."

The article also detailed a poll that was completed by the Public Religion Research Initiative (PRRI) which stated, "more than half of white Evangelical's report feeling concerned about America's declining white population." How are Christians of color supposed to feel about those statistics in this day and age, knowing that some of our brothers and sisters in Christ still feel this way when it comes to race and dominance in America? The first feeling that comes to mind for me is true sadness. The fact that people still have the same feelings and views in this season leads me to believe that true deliverance from the old demons of our history has yet to happen.

When I first came across this particular article, I didn't quite know if I wanted to touch on this topic. I did not want to come across as singling out any one group or causing any rifts or division, especially when it comes to the church. But after much prayer, I could not sit back and be silent in the face of what we know is just wrong, as the body of Christ we have to start to become who God has called us to be, unified, truthful, full of his wisdom, full of compassion and his love. So the truth has to be revealed in order for us to be totally free to be all of those things that he has called his body to be.

No matter what side of the argument you may support, we know what the Bible says about this issue, and this kind of treatment against immigrants is just plain wrong. The most tragic part of the entire situation and the policies of this current administration is the fact that two innocent children died in U.S. custody. Although we are a country of laws that need to be followed, as Christians, we do not get to use fear as an excuse to become inhumane. Speaking of being inhumane, let's go back to humanity and compare that with the choice to be a nation that is inhumane. According to Dictionary.com 'inhumane' means," not humane; lacking humanity, kindness, compassion" When I hear the word 'inhumane,' it makes me think of the 85,000 children in Yemen who have been starved to death and the many more that will die from starvation. As Christians, we all should be concerned about this crisis, but are we? In 2019, our government was in the middle of a shutdown because of politics. As Christians, we should have been concerned and praying for the people that were directly impacted by this hypocrisy and recognize that they are real people with families and real-life problems. If you are a believer, and at this point of time, you are continuing to sit quietly or continue to support what you know to be so wrong, once again you may have to go back to the source for reflection, guidance and redirection to assure that you are and remain in the will of God. *Ephesians 5:17* says, "Therefore do not be foolish and thoughtless, but understand and firmly grasp what the will of the Lord is."

As Christians, sometimes we become so saturated and overwhelmed in our own circumstances that it is hard to focus on anything else that's going on all around us. We have to continue to be fervent in prayer, staying close to the source, so we will not become desensitized to the suffering of others. We must be aware of the strategy of the enemy to keep us so engaged in conflict that we start to lose our sensitivity and our obligation to humanity; in which my brothers and sisters in Christ is a part of our obligation as Christians. We have to realize as a people we cannot be who God has called us to be without caring about the issues surrounding others. We come from different backgrounds, cultures, traditions, political affiliations, religions and social economic statuses, but we all have the same basic needs in order to survive and be a productive member of society.

The first thing that comes to mind when I think about our common needs is Maslow's hierarchy of needs which is, "a motivational theory in psychology comprising a five-tier model of human needs in order for us to be whole and healthy. This model was written by a man named Abraham Maslow in 1943." He broke those needs down into five different categories in a pyramid: Self-actualization: "achieving one's full potential, including creative activities; Esteem needs: prestige and feeling of accomplishment; Belongingness and love needs: intimate relationships, friends; Safety needs: security, safety and the most significant of all the needs is, Physiological needs: food, water, warmth, rest." So of course, his theory was the essential needs at the bottom of the list have to be satisfied before individuals can attend to needs higher up. Maslow's Theory reminds me that even though we are all different, we have the same common need to be whole healthy adults but the most important need that Maslow left out of the equation is that need that touches our souls and that to me is our spirituality, experiencing and having a relationship with Christ, experiencing his love, showing compassion, kindness, and empathy to one another and those in crisis, that aspect of us is what makes us human. So if we have that love of Christ within it should be very hard to reject people fleeing their country to find that security and safety, they need. It just seems very cruel and inhumane to me to build a wall to keep those in need and running from dangerous situations seeking asylum from entering. As Christians, instead of being led by falsehoods we must always allow the spirit of God to lead us to truth. *Ephesians 4:25-26* says, "Therefore, rejecting all falsehood (whether lying, defrauding, telling half-truths, spreading rumors, any such as these), speak truth each one with his neighbor, for we are all parts of the body of Christ). Be angry (at sin—at immorality, at injustice, at ungodly behavior), yet do not sin; do not let your anger (cause you shame, nor allow it to) last until the sun goes down."

I ask the question, what would Jesus do? *Ephesians 4:2* says, "With all humility and gentleness, with patience, bearing with one another in love," *Micah 6:8* says, "He has told you, O man, what is good; and what does the Lord require of you but to do justice, and to love kindness, and to walk humbly, with your God?"

CHAPTER 9

My righteousness means what?

Most people equate righteousness with being morally good, upright. The definition of 'righteousness' is, "morally right or justifiable: righteous indignation, acting in an upright, moral way; virtuous: a righteous and Godly person." Some may believe in order to be deemed righteous, we have to follow the law to the tee, no room for error always on edge, focusing on what we can and cannot do as Christians. If we are not careful, this righteousness can become a heavy weight that can become a form of bondage, where we are constantly judging others and ourselves because we are so intensively trying to follow the law and reach a certain status in Man and not Christ. This seems to be a righteousness man-made. *Philippians 3:9* says, "And be found in him, not having a righteousness of my own that comes from the law, but that which comes through faith in Christ, the righteousness from God that depends on faith." So that says it all— God's righteousness is not given to us because of what we may have done, it comes through our salvation. Once we receive Christ into our hearts, we are deemed.

Righteous and Holy because that is what he is, so if we are a part of him, that means we are the same. It's not our works that make us righteous; it's our belief and faith in him that makes us righteous. As Christians, in order for us to be free, we have to know that our righteousness is made perfect in him. Without knowledge of that truth, we will continue to walk in circles in the wilderness, living a defeated life, working tirelessly to prove that we are righteous. *Romans 4:5* says, "And to the one who does not work but believes in him who justifies the ungodly, his faith is counted as righteousness." *Romans 1:17:* "For the gospel reveals the righteousness of God that comes by faith from start to finish, just as it is written: 'The righteous will live by faith.' Once we come to the realization that our righteousness is in him, we will be able to operate within the fruits of the spirit. According to *Galatians 5:22,* "But the fruit of the Spirit (the result of His presence within us) is love (unselfish concern for others), joy, (inner) peace, patience (not the ability to wait, but how we act while waiting), kindness, goodness, faithfulness, gentleness, self-control. Against such things, there is no law."

The fruits of the spirit are intertwined with the character of God so once we accept and receive him, we begin to become new and take on his traits and character. Our new traits and character, often are developed over time through our trials and tribulations so it will be beneficial to each and every one of us to be open to the process; receive and learn from our training. We do not want to repeat the same lesson over and over again because either we didn't get it or we didn't receive it the first time, yes walking around in circles in the wilderness. *John 15:1-5* "I am the true Vine, and My Father is the vinedresser. Every branch in Me that does not bear fruit, He takes away; and every branch that continues to bear fruit, He (repeatedly) prunes, so that it will bear more fruit (even richer and finer fruit). You are already clean because of the word which I have given you (the teachings which I have discussed with you). Remain in me, and I (will remain) in you. Just as no branch can bear fruit by itself without remaining in the vine, neither can you (bear fruit, producing evidence of your faith) unless you remain in Me. I am the Vine; you are the branches. The one who remains in me and I in him bears much fruit, for (otherwise) apart from me (that is, cut off from vital union with me) you can do nothing." A broken union with him, my friends, is being cut off from the power source. Thank you, God, for letting us know that we are the righteousness of God and we are Holy because you are Holy.

I would like to leave you with some food for thought through Scripture. *Luke 18:9* says, "He also told this parable to some people who trusted in themselves and were confident that they were righteous (posing outwardly as upright and in right standing with God), and who viewed others with contempt:" *Psalm 37:6* says, "He will make your righteousness (your pursuit of right standing with God) like the light, And your judgment like (the shining of) the noonday (sun)."

CHAPTER 10

Unmasking Un-forgiveness

I often wondered why Christians have a harder time conquering un-forgiveness, more so than the nonbelievers. When the offense comes more often than not, we hold on and bury it deep, so it seems like we have forgiven the person who perpetrated the offense, but the truth is un-forgiveness still exists in our hearts. It is buried so deep that we fool ourselves into believing that we are good when we are not. If we allow it to settle in our hearts for too long, it will begin to manifest over time, and begin to start eating at the soul. Some of the symptoms that are affiliated with un-forgiveness are, trouble sleeping, thinking about the situation over and over again, inability to let it go, rehashing and talking about the situation over and over again, becoming easily angered, passive aggressive behavior with the individual that you have supposedly forgiven.

Bitterness starts to set in, and that's when it can become dangerous to your spirit, soul and body. It's similar to a developing wound that starts at Stage one, in which it presents as a bruise or reddened area.

If that small area doesn't heal in time, it will develop into a Stage two wound, which presents as a superficial break in the skin that is only on the surface. If that Stage two wound is not treated immediately, and is allowed fester, it may become a Stage three wound, which is deeper and begins to affect the subcutaneous layer (the fat layer). If you continue to ignore the wound and allow it to go without treatment, it will develop into a Stage 4 wound, and at this point, it can become life-threatening without immediate professional treatment. This wound is deep. In most cases, there is a serious loss of skin, fat, bone, tendon, or muscle tissues. This is at the point where a bad infection can settle into the wound and the bloodstream. If you allow the Stage four to go without professional treatment, it will soon develop into an unstageable wound in which, full thickness loss with exposed bone, tendons or muscle, slough or eschar (black dead tissue) may be present over parts of the wound. Chemical debridement or surgical removal is the only way to remove the necrotic tissue from the wound in order for it to have a chance of healing. If a wound becomes unstageable, normally it is directly related to severe neglect, substandard care or some underlying condition that has a direct impact on the wound.

We have to remain alert to the symptoms of un-forgiveness in our hearts. Once we become aware that some form of un-forgiveness exists in our hearts, it must be destroyed before it has a chance to take root. The first step is to recognize that you have un-forgiveness in your heart, secondly, once you recognize that you are dealing with un-forgiveness on some level, begin to drive it out through prayer, fasting and staying connected to the source. I often wonder why it is so hard for Christians to be genuine and forgive one another. We say we forgive but we continue to bring up our past hurts over and over again, never really dealing with the wound from the offense, because we are supposed to be on a solid foundation following the Word of God to a tee. We often put on a mask to cover up and pretend that all is well. We all know what the Word says about not harboring un-forgiveness in our hearts, and the impact that it can have on our lives. If we do not properly deal with those feelings, they can lead us into a dark place that is filled with bitterness, despair, depression, and if we are not careful, sickness and death. Each offense that we unknowingly bury in our hearts has the potential to reopen wounds of the past. It is so crucial that we are honest and transparent with God about all our flaws. If we continue to wear a mask to cover our true feelings and flaws, then we may need to recognize that it could be some form of pride. And we all know what the Word says comes before a fall—yes, that would be pride.

It is so ironic to me that Christians are more subject to wounding from people in the church Versus people in the world, and sometimes, it causes wounded sheep to go from pasture to pasture in search of the perfect pasture to be fed. The wounded sheep goes from church to church carrying open wounds, and they are looking to people to heal the wounds instead of going directly to the source for healing. Without complete healing, it becomes difficult to develop healthy relationships until all of the wounds festering within the wounded are completely healed. I know some people may be thinking, or perhaps saying that it all sounds well and good, but it's not that simple in all circumstances, and we know that our heavenly father is also aware of our weaknesses. God knows what it will take to get us to true forgiveness; just remember releasing forgiveness is more beneficial to you than to the person that is being forgiven. While you are in turmoil on the inside because of un-forgiveness that you have been holding onto for thirty years, the other person is living their best life.

One thing that comes to mind for me is when my father left our family and started a new life with a new family when I was around seven years old. That rejection left a gaping hole in my heart, along with a wound deep within that grew over the years. I internalized anger for years, and that anger turned into depression. According to Sigmund Freud, "Depression is anger turned inward." It took me years to realize that I had not forgiven my father, and I carried around so much anger on the inside until I was able to truly forgive him. It wasn't an easy task but it set me free. When people go through abusive situations in their childhood, sometimes, it's harder to forgive. Another sensitive topic for African Americans is our painful history of how our ancestors were brought to this country as slaves, and all the atrocities that happened during and after slavery, that ugly Jim Crow era, and all the racism that has followed that history. After an incident that happen on February 1, 2019, in which some conservative organization dug up thirty year old pictures of a male in black face along with a person dressed in a Klu Klux Klan costume that was on the Governor of Virginian's college year book page, now those pictures were horrible, disgusting, painful but those pictures were not shocking for many of us that have lived in the commonwealth for all of our lives we are painfully aware of our state's dark and ugly pass of this very thing. So whether our Governor was in the picture or not it's a part of a much bigger systemic issue that still exists today.

Everyone all over the country came out against the Governor, and rightly so, if he was in the picture. But what I hope is that everyone from both parties will equally condemn the fact that the legislators in Virginia continue to honor Robert E Lee a couple of days before Martin Luther King's birthday. I find this more appalling than the thirty-year-old pictures on that year book page. I believe by honoring this dark figure in our history that led one of the Confederate armies in the Civil War to keep a race of people enslaved, continuously reminds us of that dark and evil past. The symbolic meaning of those pictures is no worse than all of the monuments throughout the State along with all the Confederate flags that we see on people's vehicles, homes, state buildings that so vividly reminds us of this country's dark and ugly past. If it was the Governor in those pictures, he needs to be honest about where he was as a person at that time, ask for forgiveness, and move on with doing the people's business.

As a country, we are quick to judge and not forgive. We all have made mistakes in life; some mistakes are worse than others. I also believe that the media has a huge impact in the way that people respond to a situation or crisis. The public can be heavily influenced by the media's response. If they are coming down hard on a person, the public begins to gravitate to that opinion, or if an opinion is trending on social media, it becomes contagious. We have to use reason and not let others influence our own personal opinions. As Christians, we should have the same compassion as Jesus Christ, since we are made in his image. We must not let the past hinder our future and stop us from moving into our destiny. Our emotions often interfere with our decision-making skills and may hinder us from showing compassion, especially when it comes to forgiveness and giving people a second chance.

As Christians, we should not be so quick to throw people under the bus, especially if they may have made a significant change in their lives. Now don't get me wrong, I am not saying to condone the behavior but what I am saying is we all have fallen short. If the Governor is saying that he has changed, and this is the only infraction in his past dealing with this issue, then I believe he should be given another chance to prove himself further to the people of Virginia. He has done good things for the state in a short period of time with the expansion of Medicaid. He seems to be working for the people, trying to increase the minimum wage for the State to give the people more to work with. The hike in the wage is scheduled to be increased over time. I believe this is a good start but much more is needed to address the issue of poverty.

In some situations, we wrestle with forgiveness. I can remember one situation around six years ago. My family and I went to the peanut festival for the first time in Suffolk, Virginia, because my youngest son's class painted pictures that were going to be on display at the festival. When we walked into the festival, we saw all of the rides and art, so I thought this is going to be fun but after we let the kids go on a few of the rides, we started to notice people holding and waving Confederate flags. So I asked my husband, are you seeing what I am seeing? And his response was "yes". It was shocking to see that many people holding and waving Confederate flags at a public event. As we continued to walk throughout the festival, it became more and more disturbing to me, and I just wanted to get my family out of there, so we left. I told my husband that I would never take my family back to that place again. The sad fact was that the individuals waving and flashing those flags all over seemed to know it was offensive. So as I said, before those photos are symptoms of a much bigger problem, and seeing that Confederate flag and what it symbolizes is just as offensive as those pictures. They both, for me, represent a form of rebellion and hate.

With all that being said, as a people, we still have to forgive those who bring the offense, we cannot walk around feeling bitter and with a chip on our shoulder when it comes to this dark side of America that still exists. If we, do it, it only hurts us. At this point, all I know to do is continue to pray and asked God to give direction on how to enlighten those individuals that are still in the dark when it comes to what constitutes racism. Spike Lee said something on one of the morning shows that I thought was so profound. He was answering questions about his new movie and the Blackface debacle came up along with the fact that twelve Presidents owned slaves. Spike Lee said, "We have to be honest about our history so we can move forward." He was absolutely correct—we cannot ignore all the atrocities that we're committed against our ancestors many years ago with all the racism that we continue to face today. Nevertheless, we also have to let go of anything that keeps us in bondage, and un-forgiveness is one of those things that will keep us bound.

I will be honest with you it's not easy to forgive and pray for people who hate you because of the color of your skin but it's something we must do. People of God remove the masks and receive your healing. *Matthew 18:21-22* says, "Then Peter came to Him and asked, 'Lord, how many times will my brother sin against me and I forgive him and let it go? Up to seven times?' Jesus answered him, 'I say to you, not up to seven times, but seventy times seven.' "For if you forgive other people when they sin against you, your heavenly Father will also forgive you." *Matthew 6:9-15*

"Our Father who is in heaven, Hallowed be Your name. Your kingdom come; your will be done on earth as it is in heaven. Give us this day our daily bread. And forgive us our debts, as we have forgiven our debtors (letting go of both the wrong and the resentment). And do not lead us into temptation, but deliver us from evil. (For Yours is the kingdom and the power and the glory forever. Amen.)' For if you forgive others their trespasses (their reckless and willful sins), your heavenly Father will also forgive you. But if you do not forgive others (nurturing your hurt and anger with the result that it interferes with your relationship with God), then your Father will not forgive your trespasses."

Colossians 3:13 says, "Bearing graciously with one another, and willingly forgiving each other if one has a cause for complaint against another; just as the Lord has forgiven you, so should you forgive."

CHAPTER 11

God, family and the church

The family unit is as important to the church as the church is to the family unit. The family unit needs to be protected at all costs, because it is the foundation of our communities and therefore the church. Prayer is a key part of keeping the family unit bonded together. The Word of God gives us the tools that we need in order to keep our family units intact. But we have to be willing to do the work—to go the extra mile in our prayer life. We can be busy at times, making a living for our families and trying to keep our households intact, trying to fulfill duties we may have in the church and trying to attend every church event. If we are not careful, just trying to keep up with our lives can become overwhelming. Over the years, I have seen Christians who blindly become consumed with pledging their commitment and loyalty to man instead of God. So, as Christians, we must remember, even though our loyalty to the Church is important, we cannot forget the order in which our loyalty and commitment of time should be shared. I believe it should be God, family and then church. We have to be able to take care of our own households first in order to be effective in taking care of the church. *1 Timothy 3:5* says, "For if someone does not know how to manage his own household, how will he care for God's church?" So, yes, we have to put God first in order to gain the tools that are needed to be able to take care of our families, making sure that our children are equipped with everything they need to succeed and make it in this world with or without us.

For all the married Christians out there, remember to keep the relationship fresh to prevent the two of you from growing apart. You must spend quality time together outside of the church. A date night is a great way to start. I don't care if you have been married for fifty years, marriage is hard work—yes, it involves work, and you have to put in the time and effort in order to mature in the relationship over time. I would like to take this time to tell you about a true story that I witnessed as a young girl. I had a friend that I would often visit during the summer when I was around maybe eleven or twelve years old. During this time, my friend lived in the home with her mother, father, sister and her brothers. One of the reasons I enjoyed visiting this particular friend was because I enjoyed being around her fun-loving parents and that was something that I did not see a lot of in my own household because during this time my parents were divorced. It gave me some sense of hope to see a family unit that was so intact; the parents seemed to be in love, and they were always joking around with one another. It was just a breath of fresh air to see the unity in the family. Everything seemed fine for a while but once we returned to school after our summer break, I got really busy with school and other things, so it was a couple of months before I had a chance to visit them again.

Once I went back for a visit, I instantly realized that something had changed. Her mother looked very different to me. She began to dress differently; she stopped wearing pants, and from that point on, I only saw her in long skirts or dresses. She stopped wearing the makeup that she had worn in the past. During this visit, she looked like a completely different person. As a young girl, I remember thinking to myself, why is she dressing like someone's grandmother? At that time, I really didn't understand what was happening until her daughter told me her mother had recently given her life to Christ. She had joined one of the local churches, and this way of dressing was a part of her newfound salvation. She didn't appear to be the same lively, happy person that I had seen months ago. It appeared to me that the entire atmosphere in the home had changed. The husband seemed to be different, and I did not see that playful interaction between the two of them. I didn't know exactly what was going on but somehow, I knew it wasn't good. I could tell the situation was having an impact on that entire family. Not too long after that visit, I found out that the father had moved out, and the next thing I knew they were divorced. One of their sons got into a little trouble and had to do a little time in jail. It wasn't until many years later that I found out the truth about what had come between that family unit, and no, it was not God or salvation, it was something called 'religion'.

What does it truly mean to give your life to Christ and become a new creature in Christ? As Christians, it is so vital for us to know what it truly means to be righteous. It is not what you wear that deems you as righteous. The wife was misinformed about what true salvation meant, and because of her lack of knowledge about the truth, she lost her husband and the unity of her family. She was taught to change the outside but the church didn't equip her with tools needed to keep her family unit together through her transformation. The wife did not consider or recognize where her husband was during her transitional process. She didn't know to factor in his feelings, and the fact that he may have needed more of her attention and help to adapt and understand her transformation.

I believe that communication is gravely important during this process. The spouse that is being transformed must be led by the spirit to gradually settle their family into the transition. They must know that even though the Word says in *1st Corinthians 7:14*: "For the unbelieving husband is sanctified by the wife, and the unbelieving wife is sanctified by the husband: else were your children unclean; but now are they holy." He or she has to pray for guidance on how to transition the rest of the family into their new life in Christ. It may take time for the spouse to get use to the changes, but the sanctified spouse must not judge, condemn, or force their change on the spouse that has not been enlightened yet. We are to be an example, treat them with love, kindness and understanding until they can embrace and come into the knowledge of salvation. Do not be too aggressive; allow the spirit to woo that unsaved loved one and if you do not get anything else out of this chapter, please do not give the enemy room to come in and break up your marriage and destroy your family unit. The enemy will try to use the smallest things to creep in and wreak havoc in order to destroy marriages. So don't give him the opportunity. It could be something such as spending less time with your spouse because of your newfound faith that could potentially cause a rift between husband and wife. We have to pray for God to give us wisdom on how to manage our time so we will not alienate our spouses; therefore, making room for as the Bible says in *Proverbs*, the strange woman (seducing spirit) to come in and destroy your marriage. *Proverbs 7:5* says, "That they may keep thee from the strange woman, from the stranger which flattereth with her words." People of God we have to use wisdom in all things. "Say unto wisdom, Thou art my sister; and call understanding thy kinswoman:" *Proverbs 7:4*. The older women should teach the younger women, just like Naomi did for Ruth when it came to Boaz. She gave her the tools that she needed. *Ruth3:1-5* says, "Then Naomi her mother-in-law said to Ruth, "My daughter, shall I not look for security and a home for you, so that it may be well with you? Now Boaz, with whose maids you were (working), is he not our relative? See now, he is winnowing barley at the threshing floor tonight. So wash and anoint yourself (with olive oil), then put on your (best) clothes, and go down to the threshing floor; but stay out of the man's sight until he has finished eating and drinking. When he lies down, notice the place where he is lying, and go and uncover his feet and lie down. Then he will tell you what to do. Ruth answered her, 'I will do everything that you say'." Ruth followed the instructions of her elder and was rewarded for doing so—she gained a husband and wealth.

As for the wife in my story; I do not believe that God intended for her to lose her husband and break up their family unit because of religious traditions. Ladies, we have to be wise. If you give your life to Christ before your spouse, and he has not yet been enlightened to the knowledge of truth, please believe me when I say, it is not required that you change yourself on the outside in order to bring change on the inside to suit religion. Jesus Christ will do the work within, so continue to keep yourself appealing for your spouse to keep that fire in your marriage kindled and your relationship intact. You do not have to give your husband ultimatums about receiving Christ. Remember that your eyes were also closed to the light before you were chosen to see. So just continue to pray fervently and work on yourself and your own relationship with Jesus Christ, and please do not try to pressure or guilt him into attending Church with you because trust me when I say that it will fail. Just continue to show him love and live a virtuous life before him as best as you can, and please believe me when I say, we will all make mistakes but you must continue to pray, stay encouraged and let God do the rest.

One last thing, you must share the goodness of God with him at every opportunity that comes your way. I know this is a painful pill to swallow for many people that have been caught up in tradition and religion for some time now. I am so thankful that I have been so blessed over the years to have mature seasoned women of God to give me those tools that I needed to ensure that I didn't make the same mistakes over again, and they checked me whenever I was wrong when it came to my marriage.

We have to be more concerned about the right relationship with Jesus Christ Versus religiosity. I also remember thinking at some point during that situation regarding the wife in my story, if that is what transformation looked like after becoming a Christian with all that sadness, then I didn't want any part of it. But thank God for grace and revelation to the truth. I can see clearly now. We win them with love, understanding and patience.

1 Peter 3:1 says, "Likewise, wives, be subject to your own husbands, so that even if some do not obey the word, they may be won without a word by the conduct of their wives," "However, let each one of you love his wife as himself, and let the wife see that she respects her husband." *Ephesians 5:33.* "Whoever troubles his own household will inherit the wind, and the fool will be servant to the wise of heart. *Proverbs 11:29.*

Dear heavenly Father, I come before you asking that you will enlighten your people to the truth when it comes to the church and relationships. I asked that you will keep all marriages covered by the blood of Jesus, assist your people with managing their time and set forth a balance. We come against every seducing spirit that comes to tempt your people in order to destroy the family unit. In Jesus' Name, I pray, Amen.

CHAPTER 12

Experiencing the church

According to Wikipedia, the independent black churches were formed in the North in 1787, "when black members of Philadelphia's George Methodist church refused to accept segregation and discrimination within the church." "The formation of the independent church was directly related to the separatist movement, reflecting free blacks' rejection of the prejudices of their white co-religionists, led to forming the AME Church (1816), the AME Zion Church (1821), the Colored ME Church (1870) and many Baptist churches around the same time." The independent black churches were "heavily in the abolitionist movement and were "stations" for runaway slaves during the Underground Railroad."

I am one of those that can say that I was brought up in the church. We were affiliated with COGIC (Church of God IN Christ). According to Wikipedia, "The Church of God in Christ is a Pentecostal-Holiness Christian denomination with a predominantly African-American membership. The denomination reports having more than 12,000 churches and over 6.5 million members in the United States making it the largest Pentecostal church in the country. COGIC was formed in 1897 by a group of disfellowshipped Baptists, most notably Charles Price Jones and Charles Harrison Mason. They were licensed Baptist ministers in Mississippi who began teaching and preaching a Wesleyan doctrine of Christian perfection or Entire Sanctification as a second work of grace to their Baptist congregations. Mason was influenced by the testimony of an African American Methodist evangelist named Amanda Berry Smith, one of the most widely respected African-American holiness evangelist of the nineteenth century. Her life story led many African-Americans into the Holiness movement, including Mason. He testified to receiving Entire Sanctification after reading her autobiography in 1893." Charles Price Jones in June 1896 held a Holiness convention at Mt. Helen Baptist Church in Jackson, Mississippi, attended by Mason and others from several states.

Other American Baptist ministers did not respond well to the new Christian movement, especially the ministers from the south, such as Mississippi, Tennessee and Arkansas. They considered them to be controversial, so the leadership of the Mississippi State Convention of the National Baptist Convention expelled the two men and many others who embraced the Wesleyan teaching of Entire Sanctification. So, some leaders didn't want to receive and adopt the entire process of sanctification. I remember, as a young girl, from time to time, I would go to church with my cousins and they were members of a Methodist Church. I just remember the experience being like night and day compared to the experience at my home church, (Church of God in Christ), better known as a Holiness Church.

At my cousin's church the choir's musical abilities were good, the preacher preached but I really didn't see the members of that church praise God like they did at my home church. I was young so I didn't quite know what to make of the difference in the two ministries. And what really had me confused as a child was when I would see people at my cousin's church pulling out cigarettes and smoking as soon as they stepped outside the church doors. If anyone knows anything about growing up in the Church of God and Christ, it is that smoking on church grounds is a big deal. So you can imagine as a young girl how confused I was. Thank God, I have been enlightened by the truth— knowing that yes, smoking is a bad habit that is harmful to your health but it is not central to your salvation. I spent most of my childhood in a Holiness Church filled with tradition and strict rules and regulations. I am not being critical of my up-bringing in the Church of God and Christ because that foundation was crucial for my survival. According to Wikipedia,

"The Church of God in Christ became the first legally charted Pentecostal body incorporated in the United States." In 1915, a legally charted Holiness body called the Church of Christ (Holiness)

U.S.A was organized, and in 1897 Bishop C.H. Mason founded and established Church of God In Christ (COGIC). He also started the annual gatherings of COGIC members, known as the 'International Holy Convocation' that was held in Memphis Tennessee. At this yearly convocation, the members gathered for prayer, fasting, teaching, preaching, fellowship and they conducted business related to the national COGIC organization. I remember attending a meeting with our church when I was around eleven or twelve years old. We took a bus all the way from Virginia to Memphis. The conference lasted for a week, and we attended services nearly all-day long. I enjoyed the trip and the experience. I have a lot of fond memories of my childhood experiences with the church. I can vividly remember the nice dresses and suits along with the big, fancy hats that some of the women would wear to Sunday services. The men would be decked out in their nice, fresh suits, but most of all, I enjoyed the singing and seeing the saints of God catch the Holy Ghost. I enjoyed seeing the saints of God filled with the spirit of Praise, dance all over the Sanctuary that was filled with the presence of God. When I was a child, I did not fully understand the significance of Praise, now I know from experience not only is it a reverence to God but it also releases a source of freedom to the Praise. Praise has the tendency to free us from the stress of everyday life, it brings us closer to God and it is very important in the life of the believer.

Thinking back, I cannot remember a time in my childhood when I wasn't in church. I can remember my mother and me staying in church on Sundays from early morning to around three in the afternoon, and then we would go back around seven thirty for the evening service. It was a very long day but I did enjoy the experience. We ate lunch at the church and I was so in love with the fresh fried chicken and lemon pound cake. As a young girl, I was in the children's choir (The Sunshine Band). We started in the morning with Sunday school and we were placed in classes according to our ages, and I enjoyed that much. Our Church also had other services during the week, including Bible study on one night of the week, YPWW (Young People Willing Workers) on another night of the week, and yes, Friday night services every week and then back on Sunday. When I was younger, my mom and I usually went three days out of the four but when I got older, she would allow me to stay home on some of the weekdays because I had school the next morning.

I didn't understand back then why my mom made me go to church so often but now I understand her thinking clearly. She wanted me to be in the house of God to give me that foundation, and plus she was a single parent with a young daughter growing up in not the best neighborhood. Now that I am an adult with my own children, I want to protect them as much as I can. My desire for them is to know God and have a relationship with Jesus Christ. I also want them to learn how to balance their lives when it comes to family, work and whatever they may do in the ministry. As Christians, we know that it is important for us to spend time with God to develop our relationship. We have a responsibility to our families and then we have to make the time for fellowship in the house of the Lord. We have to be wise when dealing with our time, so we will not become overwhelmed, and burn out.

I would like to give you a profound quote that I read in the *Jesus Calling Enjoying Peace in His Presence* book by Sarah Young. "Don't fall into the trap of being constantly on the go. Many, many things people do in My Name have no value in My Kingdom. To avoid doing meaningless works, stay in continual communication with me. I will instruct you and teach you in the way you should go; I will counsel you with my eye upon you." *Luke 10: 41* says, "But the Lord replied to her, 'Martha, Martha, you are worried and bothered and anxious about so many things, but only one thing is necessary, for Mary has chosen the good part (that which is to her advantage), which will not be taken away from her'." I would just hate for anyone to be so busy that they miss the very thing that we seek to obtain, and that is the kingdom of God. It is so important that we realize that what we do for the kingdom is more important to God than programs, functions, meetings and conferences. They are all a part of the fellowship but sometimes, it can become a bit overwhelming if you are trying to run to every service, function and program—running to the next big event when you still have to work, raise your children, attend events outside the church, and most importantly, spend that quality time with Jesus Christ. It can become very stressful. As Christians, we have to use wisdom and balance our lives once again to ensure we do not miss the move of God. It is a part of the Shepherd's duty to guide the sheep and protect the sheep from self-destruction, among many other things.

I gave you a synopsis of my experience with church when I was a young child. Now let's move on to my experience after that point, starting with me leaving the Church I grew up in because after a certain age, I just wanted to venture out to see if there was any place out there where I could go and feel free. I use the word 'free' because at times, growing up in the church, we had to abide by strict standards as far as how we dressed was concerned. It was heavily frowned on for women to wear pants and makeup. Most of the women that I saw had on long skirts or dresses they had to be a certain length without splits. I was once chastised for having a split on one side of my skirt. It took place during a Sunday service, and I had on a suit, the length of the skirt was appropriate but I was chastised by one of the elders in the church for having a split on one side of the skirt. I remember it just like it was yesterday, and it threw me for a loop because she was a sweet person—one of the nicer seasoned women in the church. I don't know if it was the way she approached me with the tongue-lashing or the fact that she scolded me in front of others. I am not exactly sure but all

I know is that I felt like I didn't belong, so I left the church for a little while. I remember telling my mother about the incident, and how I was hurt and I wasn't going back to that church again. Of course, once I grew up and matured, I got over it, and I love that mother dearly now. And the truth is, after my mother addressed the issue with her, she was heartbroken and apologetic. She wasn't even aware that she had offended me, and this is exactly why the seasoned women in Christ must be attentive to the needs of the babes in Christ.

The young ladies that come into the church have a need to be loved and nurtured, not judged and frowned upon. It is up to us to pray for them and love them into the kingdom, not judge them and make them run away from the church. Our goal is to aid in helping them to mature in Christ after he draws them into his kingdom. We have to be aware of the generation that we now find ourselves living in. I remember a time growing up, when we showed up to church in our Sunday best—the young men in suits and ties, while the young women wore their nice dresses and the older women wore their sassy hats. In this day and age, the young people come to the house of the Lord dressed down and comfortably looking fly. We should be able to serve God while being comfortable at the same time. When I was growing up, things were more traditional Versus now when the younger generation can look good and be comfortable at the same time.

I went to a leadership conference many years ago, and something that the hosting pastor said about the church was profound; as far as the Church being behind the times and needs to first catch up to current times in order to be better equip to serve in the current season that we are living in. The black church today does wonderful things for the kingdom, especially when it comes to civil rights and causes of justice. In the early part of the twentieth century that the key civil rights organizations such as the NAACP were formed. The black Church since the start has been the backbone of the African-American community, to this day.

I just heard a story of an African-American church that went on a fast and prayed for twenty-one days and then raised enough money to pay off the tuitions of multiple African-American students. It was so touching to see the reactions of the young people when they received the news that their tuition would be paid in full. It is the duty of the church to use some of the money collected by the members to assist in helping the poor, the widows, and the community. I believe that this plays a big role in building up the kingdom of God. My perspective is we cannot draw the people in to help build up the kingdom of God without love and compassion. We have to do more than just say 'I will be praying for you'. We have to put forth real action in order to move the people. If a person is hungry, feed them before you minister to them—show them that you care. When people see that the church really cares about their pain and suffering, that will eventually draw them to visit the church, and then we pray the spirit of God with his word will draw them into the kingdom of God. *Acts 28:31* says "Proclaiming the kingdom of God and teaching about the Lord Jesus Christ with all boldness and without hindrance."

Now let's take a look at the White evangelical church, according to the Evangelical Evolution: 6 key events for Christian denomination since it began, written by Ken Mandel. "The evangelical movement originated within Protestantism and is rooted in the concept of salvation through atonement, or ultimately, an individual's faith. Evangelical Christians believe in being "born again" and in the Bible as God's words. The National Association of Evangelicals was formed in 1942 as a response to Pastor Harold John Ockenga's call for "neo-evangelicalism" to identify a distinct movement within self-identified fundamentalist Christianity, It described the mood of positivism and non-militancy that characterized that generation. The group included other denominations such as, "Pentecostal and Holiness and independent ministries. Although there are many different Denominations, races, evangelical Christians are unified when it comes to their core beliefs. That you must be "born-again or saved", believe in the Bible as God's inspired Word to humankind, perfect in truth in the original text. It is the final authority in all matters of doctrine and faith above all human authority," according to EvangelicalBeliefs.com. We believe, "the work of Jesus on the cross, through his death and resurrection, is the only source of salvation and forgiveness of sins." According to Prayerfoundation.com, "People can do nothing to earn their way to heaven. Instead, as Great Commission's call to share with the world the Christian message of salvation through Christ, and to be publicly baptized as a confession of faith. And finally, they believe that there will be a rapture in the end times in which the church will be caught up with Christ before the Great Tribulation, leaving the nonbelievers behind to suffer on Earth."

According to Pew Research Center, most believers, but not all, believe there will be a rapture. My experience with the white evangelical church has mostly been refreshing. I have had the experience of attending a charismatic white Christian church with a multicultural membership and a non-charismatic multicultural church, and the worship was authentic in both ministries. The worship teams were completely different but it seemed they produced the same effect. The Word was on point, and the presence of God was in the buildings. I attended one of the churches for some time and I was leaning towards becoming a member but there were a couple of things that turned me off from joining this ministry. For one, they appeared to be too political. It was during the 2008 Presidential election; the year President Obama was elected to office. And during every service, politics seemed to be a hot topic of conversation.

I will never forget on one Sunday before the election, the pastor was preaching to the congregation the importance of voting for our biblical principles during the upcoming election, no matter how historic the election would be. It was obvious that she was trying to steer the congregation in one direction and it wasn't in the direction of President Obama being elected. He wasn't the right choice for the country because some of his policies were contrary to our biblical principles. Even though he professed to be a Christian, his policies leaned too far to the left of the political spectrum. I felt that all the discussion about politics was starting to become one big distraction. One other thing that was concerning to me was the fact that even though it was a multicultural, multiracial ministry, the pulpit and leadership in the ministry did not reflect that fact. I don't believe that it was intentional that all of the leadership in the ministry were of one race but it does give some insight into the fact that the church has some real work to do when it comes to race. I would like to leave you with a prayer from (Uninterrupted talks with God written by Tiwana L. Adams) "God we repent right now for hindering anyone from coming to you because of our actions. We thank you now for the winds of change blowing away anything that is not like you. It is in the name of Jesus, we pray. Amen."

CHAPTER 13

Blurred boundaries: Are you in or out?

Where are we in this day and age as Christians? Are we closer to conforming to the things of the world, or are we closer to conforming to the kingdom of God; or are we doing our own thing and living life on our own terms? Are we walking a tightrope with our eternity or playing a dangerous game of Russian roulette with our souls? Are we being who God has called us to be and taking care of our Father's business and furthering his kingdom by our actions? Are we setting a good example for our children; being aware they are watching our every move? Or are we just going through the motions of being religious?

A word that I received from the book, *Jesus Calling Enjoying Peace in His Presence*, written by Sarah Young, said it best, when dealing with religion, and I would like to share: "Men tend to multiply duties in their observance of religion. This practice enables them to give me money, time, and work without yielding up to me what I desire the most—their hearts. Rules can be observed mechanically, once they become habitual, they can be followed with minimal effort and almost no thought. These habit-forming rules provide a false sense of security, lulling the soul into a comatose condition."

I also believe we have to be so very careful when we are working to know why we are working and what the common goal of our labor is. We have to make sure our motives are pure by pleasing God, and not man. It is important that we are working to build up the kingdom of God and not man's ego. Because of his grace we do not have to earn our way into the kingdom by completing vain works, nor do we have to fight for positions and titles to be seen by God. He always has his eyes on each and every one of us. I have often wondered why titles and positions are so important especially in the black church. Could it be that because of our history, we may have a yearning to feel important and to be recognized? I am not really sure; it is just a thought.

We have to get delivered from people and our own selfish motives, realizing that we are all ambassadors of Christ so we have to represent him at all times—whether we are in church, at work, at home and yes, even on the street. If you pass someone on the street, make eye contact, give them a smile. Someone may be having a bad day, and your smile with the love of Christ attached to it, will lift them up and brighten their day. It is so important that we stay vigilant to the things of God and stay in tune with what needs to be done for the kingdom.

If he is leading you to pick up the phone and call that person that has been on your mind, be obedient and make the call—that person may be struggling and need prayer or encouragement. When was the last time you prayed for someone that was sick or fed someone that was hungry or visited someone in jail or prison? *Matthew 25:35-40* tells us, " For I was hungry, and you gave Me something to eat; I was thirsty, and you gave Me something to drink; I was a stranger, and you invited Me in, I was naked, and you visited Me (with help and ministering care); I was in prison, and you came to Me (ignoring personal danger). Then the righteous will answer Him, 'Lord, when did we see you hungry, and feed you, or thirsty, and give you something to drink? And when did we see you as a stranger, and invite you in, or naked, and clothe you? And when did we see you sick, or in prison, and come to you?' The King will answer and say to them, 'I assure you and most solemnly say to you, to the extent that you did it for one of these brothers of Mine, even the least of them, you did it for Me'."

Have we forgotten the very basics of love? Reading this Scripture helps me to take a look at myself and where I am in my walk with Christ. How often do I follow this command when opportunity presents itself? It really makes me want to do better and be more focused on the things of God and less focused on the things of the world. I believe sometimes we are tested to see what we will do in certain circumstances.

For instance, I have an example that I would like to share. One day, my business partner and I were going about our day, and my partner had just returned from lunch and she noticed a strange man lying on the ground right behind her office window. She came to my office to tell me, so we went back to her office and looked out the window and the man was still lying outside on the ground, he was writing in a notebook; He was a young man with dark hair. He looked disheveled and cold, so I told my partner to open the window to see if he needed anything. He told us in a soft voice that he had just been kicked out of a friend's home, and he was writing down names of people that may have been able to help him. He said he was going to head to another friend to see if he could take him in for a few days. She asked him if we could help him in any way, and he proceeded to say in a soft voice, "I could use some food." I tell you that really broke my heart. My partner went over to the nearest fast-food place and returned with his food, meanwhile, I decided to run over to the nearest ATM to get out money to give to the young man. But by the time I returned, he was gone. I went back outside the building and checked the front, back and side, and he was nowhere in sight. My partner reminded me that when she asked him if he needed anything, his response was food. At that time, one Scripture came to mind. *Hebrews 13:2*: "Do not forget to show hospitality to strangers, for by so doing, some people have shown hospitality to angels without knowing it."

I am just saying you never know who or what God is going to put in your path. Oh, and by the way, he did tell us his name—it was Stefan. I was curious, so I looked up the meaning of his name and the origin of the name Stefan: "From the Latin Stephanus, which is from the Greek Stephanos, a name derived from stephanous (a crown, a garland). The name is borne in the Bible by St Stephen, one of the seven chosen to assist the apostles, and the first Christian martyr." When you find yourself distracted, often times we have to refocus our attention back to the things of God. I know we can all do better. I have another story to share with you about the humanity of man, and this story doesn't end so well. It was the beginning of April 2019. I was off for a couple of days, and upon returning to work, I entered my office building and it appeared to be a person at the other end of the hallway lying down in front of the side door. I wasn't sure about what I was seeing because the door was some distance away. So I proceeded to enter into my suite, and maybe three hours later, one of our employees called into the office to say she could not gain access to the building because there were multiple officers in the front and on the side of the building, and they had the building blocked off with crime tape. Apparently, a homeless man was lying in front of one of the entrances to the building and he was deceased. I was so disturbed by the news because apparently this person had been seen in the same spot and position three to four days before he had been pronounced dead. So that meant that there was a very good possibility that this person had been dead for more than four days without anyone knowing. The first thing that came to my mind was that he died alone, and he did not have anyone to comfort him.

How is it that in one of the richest countries in the world, so many people are homeless? I know some people who are homeless, are dealing with mental disorders but nonetheless, this is not an excuse for them to be ignored. This man lay dead for at least three to four days, and no one knew, until one of the occupants of the building who saw the man lying in the same exact spot for three days became concerned and called the manager of the building for the second time to report that she believed the individual was deceased. Finally, the building manager contacted the authorities. The fact that everyone was going about their daily routines, and no one thought to investigate further to see if this, man who was in the same spot for at least three days was okay. So yes, we have to make a conscious effort to do better.

I really believe this is a call to the people of God to do better and to get back to our first love. We have to stay focused so we can recognize the plays out of the enemy's playbook and be prepared for every assignment of the enemy against our lives. He wants to move the people of God backwards not forward, so he dangles many shiny objects pertaining to the world in front of the believer, hoping that one day we will take the bait. We are living in a world that is full of chaos and distractions. We cannot and must not give into the temptations that threaten to derail us from our walk with Christ.

As Christians, we have to be so careful as to what we feed our spirits—things such as what we watch on television and what we take in on social media. Social media can be used as a great tool but it can also be used as a wicked outlet to promote evil. You have people hiding behind social media outlets where they can say all kinds of hateful things without consequence. The modern day terminology for this type of coward is internet troll. According to Wikipedia, an internet troll "is a person who starts quarrels or upsets people on the internet to distract and sow discord by posting inflammatory and digressive, extraneous, or off-topic messages in an online community with the intent of provoking readers into displaying emotional responses and normalizing tangential discussion, whether for the troll's amusement or a specific gain." It sounds demonic to me.

As Christians, we have to be aware of the tactics of the enemy to draw us into such behavior, even if our intentions are good, we cannot entertain such behavior and get down into the mire with this evil that has saturated our society. The only way to fight this evil is with prayer, fasting and with the Word of God. *Ephesians 6:12* tells us, "For we wrestle not against flesh and blood, but against principalities, against powers, against the rulers of the darkness of this world, against spiritual wickedness in high places." We have to be vigilant when it comes to the devices of the enemy and the things that are used to draw us far away from the things of God. It may start off very subtle, maybe you stop reading the Word every day, and then all of a sudden, you go from praying once a day to praying every other day. Before you know it, you are attending church less and less. And all of a sudden, you look up and you are going back to your old lifestyle, drinking more frequently and instead of attending church and hanging out with your Christians friends, you begin attending or having social events that mirror your past before you were enlightened by the truth. You begin to feel a sense of conviction, but you ignore that unction that is tugging at you so desperately, trying to get you back on track. You begin to rationalize in your mind that you're ok because the blessings are continuing to flow in your life but don't be fooled by the enemy; one of his strategies is making us think we are ok when we are not.

Romans 12:2 tells us, "And do not be conformed to this world (any longer with its superficial values and customs), but be transformed and progressively changed (as you mature spiritually) by the renewing of your mind (focusing on godly values and ethical attitudes), so that you may prove (for yourselves) what the will of God is, that which is good and acceptable and perfect (in His plan and purpose for you)."

Let me tell you, my brothers and sisters, nothing in this life is worth us turning back and losing our souls, so keep moving forward with Christ. *Proverbs 21:2-3* says, "Every man's way is right in his own eyes. But the Lord weighs and examines the hearts (of people and their motives). To do righteousness and justice is more acceptable to the Lord than sacrifice (for wrongs repeatedly committed)." You're a single Christian and all of a the sudden, you meet someone that appears to be perfect for you, so you go out with this person a couple of times. You rationalize in your mind, it's ok to go out to a movie or maybe have a little dinner to get to know each other. You're on your third date and now you feel comfortable in each other's presence, so you begin to let your guard down. And all of a sudden, by the end of the third date, you exchange an innocent good night's kiss. You begin to rationalize in your mind again that the quick peck on the lips is harmless. Then all of sudden, the fourth date has come and gone, and you wake up the next morning full of shame and guilt because when you look to your right, there is that harmless date lying beside you uncovered. If this is your situation, fret not, because we serve a merciful and forgiving God.

As Christians, we must realize that one of the enemy's strategies is to study and target all our vulnerabilities, so he can find ways to distract us and keep us off our game. He wants to take us as far away from our assignment as possible, and he will use anything and anyone to do so. If you are single and you're lonely, he will probably use that. If you're married and you're having difficulties in your marriage, he will probably use that. So why do we give him the ammunition needed against us. Do not give him an opening to infiltrate your life. If you leave the door or window cracked, he will try to enter. It is so crucial for every believer to have a sound relationship with Jesus Christ and the baptism of the Holy Spirit. If you're single and someone comes along that you may be interested in, go to your source. He will lead you, guide you and give you insight to help you discover if that particular person is the right person for you. He will keep you alert and will lead you away from any imposters that the enemy sets before you, and while you're waiting on your soulmate, pray that God will keep you in perfect peace. We have to be careful when it comes to putting ourselves in tempting situations. If you are single and you know you are having feelings and urges that you may not be able to control, then you may not want to date until you are delivered from those urges. *James 1:13-16* says, "Let no one say when he is tempted, 'I am being tempted by God' (for temptation does not originate from God, but from our own flaws); for God cannot be tempted by (what is) evil, and He Himself tempts no one. But each one is tempted when he is dragged away, enticed and baited (to commit sin) by his own (worldly) desire (lust, passion). Then when the illicit desire has conceived, it gives birth to sin; and when sin has run its course, it gives birth to death. Do not be misled, my beloved brothers and sisters."

Now don't get me wrong. I am not saying that since you are a Christian, you should not date. But what I am saying is that you have to stay focused and keep your eyes on Christ to ensure that you are not deceived. And please, young ladies, know your value. If you know your value, you will not settle for less. We must realize that the church should be setting the example for the world with its influence, instead of the world influencing the church. We have to make a choice as to who we are going to follow, and we need to stay close to the source in order to stand against temptation and make the right choice. If we happen to get it wrong from time to time, fret not, his mercy is renewed each day. So if you fall down, repent, get back up, and move forward in Christ. And please, do not let the enemy use your guilt to distract you and keep you from your assignment. "The steadfast love of the Lord never ceases; his mercies never come to an end; they are new every morning; great is your faithfulness." *Lamentations 3:22-23*, *Psalm 139:23-24* says, "Search me (thoroughly), O God, and know my heart; Test me and know my anxious thoughts; and see if there is any wicked or hurtful way in me, and lead me in the everlasting way." *Psalm 37: 23-24* says, "The steps of a (good and righteous) man are directed and established by the Lord, And He delights in his way (and blesses his path). Because the Lord is the One who holds his hand and sustains him."

Dear Lord, help us to stay connected to the source, so we will not stray away from your kingdom. Help us to stay in direct communication with you, continually seeking your face for guidance, allowing us to see the enemy even when he is faraway. In Jesus' name, I pray. Amen.

CHAPTER 14

A Shepherd's heart

"The Lord is my Shepherd (to feed, to guide and to shield me), I shall not want. He lets me lie down in green pastures; He leads me beside the still and quiet waters. He refreshes and restores my soul (life); He leads me in the paths of righteousness for His namesake. Even though I walk through the (sunless) valley of the shadow of death, I fear no evil, for you are with me; your rod (to protect) and your staff (to guide), they comfort and console me. You prepare a table before me in the presence of my enemies. You have anointed and refreshed my head with oil; My cup overflows. Surely goodness and mercy and unfailing love shall follow me all the days of my life, And I shall dwell forever (throughout all my days) in the house and in the presence of the Lord." *Psalm 23*.

I was at an Intercessory prayer meeting some years ago. There was this graceful, sweet, humorous, seasoned woman of God who was so full of wisdom leading the meeting. During the prayer, I remember her praying for God to give pastors a Shepherd's heart. Let's dive into what this phrase means. According to Dictionary.com, the definition of 'Shepherd' is, "a person who herds, tends, and guards sheep"; "a person who protects, guides, or watches over a person or group of people"; "a member of the clergy, the Shepherd, Jesus Christ, to tend or guard as a shepherd: to shepherd the flock"; "to watch over carefully."

If you look at all the different descriptions of the word, 'Shepherd,' they all have one thing in common. And that is—the duty of the Shepherd is to protect first, then lead and guide the sheep. We have a good understanding about the Shepherd. Now let's take a look at the word, 'heart'. According to Dictionary.com, one of the definitions of the heart is, "the center of the total personality, especially with reference to intuition, feeling, or emotion: In your heart, you know I'm an honest man"; "the center of emotion, especially as contrasted to the head as the center of the intellect: His head told him not to fall in love, but his heart had the final say"; "capacity for sympathy, feeling; affection: His heart moved him to help the needy"; "the vital or essential part; core: the heart of the matter."

A pastor is considered to be a shepherd over the people of God, and I know for them, that cannot be an easy task. So they do need to be equipped with that Shepherd's heart which symbolizes a leader after his own heart—a leader who no matter what, will be led by God into their destiny to fulfill the will of God. David comes to mind, yes, even with all his flaws, God still looked on him as a man after his own heart.

He knew all of his flaws, what kind of heart he had on the inside, and exactly what kind of leader he would be. *Acts13:22* says, "And when he had removed him, he raised up unto them David to be their king; to whom also he gave their testimony, and said, I have found David the son of Jesse, a man after mine own heart, which shall fulfil all my will."

Not just anyone can lead the sheep. A leader needs that love of Christ on the inside, along with a natural gift of compassion and a hunger to serve others and to be able to see people through the eyes of God. It will take a special close relationship with God in order to see people the way he sees them. I do not believe it is something that you can learn or be taught but it is something they are born with, and is developed over time. Yes, they are chosen for the imperative task of leading the people of God. In order to be the leader that God has called them to be, whether it's in your job, at your place of business, in your household, and especially if you are a pastor in the house of God, you must accept and learn how to become a servant first. It is your duty to serve the individuals that God has given you charge over. It is your responsibility while they are in your care to make sure they are being cared for, making sure they are spiritually fed if you are a pastor. God has placed them in your care because he knows you are up for this task. If you are an employer, you also have the task of being a servant first; serving your employees, you have a responsibility to make sure your employees are safe while they are under your supervision;

making sure they are paid for their labor, ensuring they are following all of the policies and procedures of the company. You must be alert to the potential that is in each individual while also recognizing and assisting them in developing any special talents and or skills for them to be successful in fulfilling their assignments. Pastors have similar responsibilities over their flock but they bear the burden of looking after souls, and that seems to me to be a daunting task.

As Christians, we should be mindful of the burdens that the pastors have to take on and make it our business not to cause undue stress with our words and actions—avoid using words to run the leader down with conversations, spreading rumors and lies, being disrespectful even when it comes to your tone when you are addressing a concern or problem. We have to be respectful to our leaders at all times showing disrespect to the individual that God has put in charge over watching over your soul and giving you nourishment doesn't seem too wise. Don't get me wrong, I am not saying that leaders always get it right because we know that they are human, and they don't always get it right. We have to respect the office and the anointing, not just when it comes to the pastor, but anyone who has been anointed by God. *Psalm 105:15* says, "Do not touch my anointed ones; do my prophets no harm." *Hebrews 13:17* says, "Obey them that have the rule over you, and submit yourselves: for they watch for your souls, as they that must give account, that they may do it with joy, and not with grief: for that is unprofitable for you."

If you have an issue with something that your leader is doing or may have done, go to God in prayer, tell him your concerns, and pray that God will reveal to him or her if they have committed an error in any way. We have to realize that as long as we are in this flesh, we are going to make mistakes. But the most important thing is that we recognize the errors of our ways and repent. Our leaders are not immune to this fact. If you are human, you will make mistakes at some point in time. I have been an employer for over ten years now, and it has not been an easy task. But I do know that it is a huge responsibility. You are literally responsible for the well-being of the clients and staff. The one thing that my partner and I have realized during this process is that we had to become servants first, making sure everything was well with our employees and customers. I say it in that order because if the staff's needs are lacking, how will they be equipped to take care of the client's needs? It is just as important for the pastors to take care of the needs of the flock, so they in turn, can be equipped to take care of the needs of the kingdom.

One thing that I have witnessed over the years that really gives me an unsettling feeling is when I see and hear the people of God put the pastors and leaders on a pedestal, lifting them up far beyond God. We have to make sure that we do not cross the line into worshipping man instead God. Now don't get me wrong, it's ok to honor and love your pastor, but do not set them up for a fall by turning them into an idol. An idol is anything or anyone that you put before God. Pastors have to be so very careful that they do not get so caught up in admiration to the point of failing to recognize when a person has crossed the line. We all are familiar with *Exodus 34:14*, "For thou shalt worship no other god: for the Lord, whose name is Jealous, is a jealous God."

Another danger that everyone in leadership should beware of is the spirit of pride. According to Dictionary.com, the definition of pride is, "a high or inordinate opinion of one's own dignity importance, merit, or superiority, whether as cherished in the mind or as displayed in bearing, conduct, etc." Pride is one of the six things that the Lord hates. According to *Proverbs 6:16-17,*. "These six things the Lord hates; indeed, seven are repulsive to Him: A proud look (the attitude that makes one overestimate oneself and discount others), a lying tongue, and hands that shed innocent blood." My belief is that we all have a measure of pride on the inside that needs to be checked from time to time. Sometimes, I believe we have the tendency to make every attempt to deny or suppress any pride we may have, deep down on the inside. I hear people from time to time say that they are confident, and that's all well and good, but we have to be careful that we do not cross the line and move from self-confidence into pride.

According to Dictionary.com, self-confidence means, "belief in oneself and one's powers or abilities; self-confidence; self-reliance; assurance." It is ok for us to be confident about who we are in Christ

Jesus, and as a person but in doing so, we do not want to become prideful. One way to avoid pride is to stay grounded in him by staying connected to the source. I have witnessed ministries crumble under the heavy weight of pride, and don't kid yourself, the enemy will use that thing that's down on the inside of us against us because every now and then it rises up to the surface. That is why we should always check our motives to see if they are pure, and appreciate the trials and tribulations because they are a part of the purification process.

As discussed before, every good leader should be attentive to the needs of the people that they are responsible for leading. That includes knowing where the members of your ministry are economically. For instance, if your ministry is smack in the middle of a low income neighborhood, and most of your members are already struggling and living below the poverty level, I do not believe it is okay to put unnecessary pressure on them when it comes to giving. Yes, I do believe they need to be taught the principles of giving and the importance of honoring the Word of God when it comes to paying their tithes and offering and all the benefits that come with giving but people should not be forced or pressured into giving. If the pastor has to beg and plead with the people of God to do what the Word of God requires us to do, then something maybe lacking as far as trust is concerned. We should always check our motives as to why we give. *2 Corinthians 9:7* teaches us, "Let each one give (thoughtfully and with purpose) just as he has decided in his heart, not grudgingly or under compulsion, for God loves a cheerful giver (and delights in the one whose heart is in his gift)."

One thing that really bothered me while growing up in the church was, sometimes, the leaders would ask people to get into different lines according to the amount of money they could give. If you had a hundred dollars, you would get into the hundred dollar line. I never could quite understand the rationale behind the money lines, and even to this day, you have some ministries that continue to practice this method of giving. Another ritual that made me uncomfortable is when the leader taking up the offering would ask that everyone who was able to give a hundred dollars raise their hand or stand, and those individuals would raise their hands. Then they would ask for everyone who could give fifty dollars or more to raise their hands, and those people would get up and take their offering to the altar. And last but not the least, they would call for everyone else to bring their offering to the table. I felt very uneasy and wondered if anyone else felt uncomfortable, not to mention the people that truly did not have the hundred or fifty dollars to give. The Word says in *Matthew 6:4*, "so that your giving may be in secret. Then your Father, who sees what is done in secret, will reward you."

Now we know that this particular Scripture is referring to charity and giving to the poor but it sounds crystal clear that when it comes to giving, we do not give to be seen and to receive approval from man. We should be giving from our hearts and out of obedience to God. Therefore no one should have to stand in hundred-dollar lines or raise your hand to reveal your offering amount. If God tells us through his word to give in secret as far as charity to the poor is concerned, then in my opinion, what we give in reverence to God should be between the giver and God. This is not a competition of who can give the most.

Now let's dive into a very touchy subject. Prosperity theology, according to Wikipedia, is "(sometimes referred to as the prosperity gospel, the health and wealth gospel, the gospel of success, or seed faith) is a religious belief among some Christians, who hold that financial blessings and physical well-being are always the will of God for them, and that faith, positive speech, and donations to religious causes will increase one's material wealth. Prosperity theology views the Bible as a contract between God and humans: if humans have faith in God, he will deliver security and prosperity." This movement was started during the Healing Revivals of the 1950s in the United States. Some people have linked the "origins of its theology to the New Thought movement which began in the 19th century." This teaching was next interlinked into the "Word of Faith" movement and the televangelism movement in the 1980s, and later adopted into the Pentecostal Movement and Charismatic Movement in the United States and throughout the world. I believe It's ok to preach and teach about prosperity as long as the entire Word of God is being taught, including the part about sin, hell, and the grave. We all want to hear the prosperity part but it is also important that we know the entire truth of how to live a life that's pleasing to God, and leaders have to be so very careful in only preaching about prosperity. We know that seed time and harvest is in the word but it really has to be taught in a way that does not come across as selling the gospel and promises of God. The gospel of Christ cannot be bought and paid for because he already paid the price on calvary for us to receive the fullness of his promises. I have heard the good, the bad, and the ugly when it comes to giving. The good was the leaders that truly followed the Word of God and were able to articulate the principles of seed time and harvest without being demanding and or pushy. The bad are the leaders that try to guilt or pressure people into giving instead of trusting God. The ugly is the video of leaders running across an altar covered in money, anointing the money along the way. I don't know-it just didn't seem quite right-it almost came across as a performance. Let's keep it real. We all need money to live in this world, and we all desire nice things, and yes, the Word does tell us that he will give us the desires of our heart but we cannot let money consume our hearts. 1Timothy 6: 10 (AMP) says, "For the love of money [that is, the greedy desire for it and the willingness to gain it unethically] is a root of all sorts of evil, and some by longing for it have wandered away from the faith and pierced themselves [through and through] with many sorrows." We all know the Scriptures that tell to ask in prayer and we will receive but let's not be fooled into thinking that those scriptures are about seeking and asking for things in vain that will only benefit our lives alone. If you're only thinking of yourself and your desires, then you are missing the entire point of gaining wealth. All roads should lead back to the Kingdom of God. I recently read a paragraph from the book *Jesus Calling,* and it made reference to leaders who use guilt to pressure the people of God, and I would like to share this word with you. "I approve of you continuously, for I see you cloaked in My Light, arrayed in My righteousness. There is no condemnation for those who are clothed in Me! That is why I abhor the use of guilt as a means of motivation among Christians. Some pastors try to whip their people to work harder, but the end does not justify the means. Guilt-evoking messages can undermine the very foundation of grace in a believer's heart. A pastor may feel successful when his people are doing more, but I look at their hearts. I grieve when I see grace eroding, with weeds of anxious works creeping in. I want you to relax in the assurance of My perfect Love. The law of My Spirit of Life has freed you from the law of sin and death."

Now let's go back and talk about sowing seeds and reaping your harvest. When it comes to sowing, sometimes it may take some time before you are able to see the manifested harvest after sowing your seed but don't get discourage if you released the seed then believe you will receive the harvest. I want the people of God to just keep praying, believing and standing on the word of God. There are many different ways to sow a seed, for example, you can sow into someone else's life blessing them with your time, with encouragement and at times, financially.

We just have to be attentive to the spirit of God and how he is leading us to give because you may be that person, he uses to answer someone else's prayer. Will you be willing and ready to be obedient and answer the call? It is so crucial that we know the Word of God for ourselves, and that we have an authentic relationship with Jesus Christ, in order to hear him clearly even when it comes to giving. *Matthew 18:19* says, "Again I say to you, if two of you agree on earth about anything they ask, "it will be done for them by my Father in heaven"." *Matthew 21:22* says, "And whatever you ask in prayer, you will receive, 'if you have faith'." *Mark 11:24:* "For this reason, I am telling you, whatever things you ask for in prayer (in accordance with God's will), believe (with confident trust) that you have received them, and they will be given to you."

I was in my car one day on my way home from work, and I was listening to one of the Gospel radio hosts, and the topic of conversation was whether or not it was appropriate for a renowned celebrity pastor to wear a pair of four thousand-dollar shoes. I do not believe that there is anything wrong with pastors obtaining wealth and living comfortable lives, as long as the wealth and comfort is not built on the backs of the poor and the people who are a step away from poverty. I would like to give you an example of that very thing. For instance, you are a leader and God has chosen you to preach the gospel all over the country, and you have many churches that you oversee. Now you have scheduled to take your private plane to fly to one of the churches that you oversee, and this particular ministry is small, and the ministry is located in the center of an impoverished area. Is it then okay for the pastor of the church that is receiving the visit from the overseer, to ask his congregation to raise the money for the plane's fuel? My answer would be 'no,' and I will tell you why I feel this way. If God has blessed you with wealth to live a comfortable life, and he has even provided the means for you to obtain your own private plane to travel the world to minister the gospel, then surely, he has already made the provision for the fuel without bankrupting the people of God who are already struggling and are in need themselves. If anyone is wondering, yes, this is a true story that transpired in a ministry that I attended some years ago.

The leaders have to be so in tune with the heartbeat of God that they will be equipped to diagnose the needs of the people of God. *Luke 12:48*: "But the one who did not know it and did things worthy of a beating, will receive only a few (lashes). From everyone to whom much has been given, much will be required; and to whom they entrusted much, of him they will ask all the more."

I would like to discuss one last issue in this chapter that is concerning to me and that would be the sanctity of the altar. The altar is supposed to be a sacred space where the spirit of God dwells. Compared to the ark of the covenant, the altar should be where the presence of God is, and in no way should the altar be used to settle conflict or get your point across when you have some type of conflict with someone in the ministry. The altar should be set apart for prayer, worship, the anointing and the Word of God. Leaders must keep themselves saturated in the presence of God to deter the flesh from rising up and crossing that line. The altar houses that ultimate power of the spirit of God and should be reverenced at all times, set apart and used for kingdom business. Some of the churches today have the house of God lit up with flashing lights and cameras, with the lighting just perfect when the men or women of God are delivering the Word of God, and for the most part, there is nothing wrong with being creative. But the church has to be careful that this does not become a distraction or come across as a performance.

I am emphasizing the topic because a friend of mine invited a guest to her church and this was one of the churches with some of the flashing lights around the altar, and after the service, her guest did inform her that all the lights were a distraction for him. The lights seemed to be a good look as far as décor was concerned, and for some, even ushering in the presence of God into the room. We just have to be very careful that something as simple as lighting does not interfere with what God is trying to do in the service. The house of God does not have to be turned into a theater with performances being delivered, in order for his spirit to move in the service and or capture the attention of the people, when the Word is flowing through the man or woman of God with the Spirit of God leading the way, deliverance will soon follow. God should always be on display, saturating the house of God. "Lights, camera and action" can quickly turn into "Lights, camera and distraction".

Dear Lord, I lift up every leader to you. Keep them covered under your wings, lead them, guide them and direct them on how to lead and care for your sheep and give them a servant's heart, along with a selfless spirit, and continue to bless them and their entire households, continue to elevate them to the highest level of your Glory that can be obtained on this earth. I pray that you will make prosperous every area of their lives and keep them from every trap of the enemy. In Jesus' name, I pray. Amen.

CHAPTER 15

Pandemic of 2020

Who could have imagined that in the beginning of 2020, the entire world would be engulfed in a vicious pandemic—yes, the rapid spread of a deadly virus that has no boundaries. Covid-19 is the name given to this silent killer that preys on the most vulnerable population, the elderly, individuals with preexisting conditions and weakened immune system. People of color have been impacted at far greater levels than other races, as well as people who are living below the poverty level. So once again, we see the impacts of poverty, poor health as well as the lack of healthcare coverage. They are all connected to the inequality in this country that occurs from years of systematic racism. How does a family that's barely making ends meet afford to eat healthy when foods that are good for us are so much more expensive? Years of unhealthy eating often take a toll on the body, sometimes causing obesity, and triggering all kinds of preexisting conditions such as diabetes, hypertension, heart disease. It's more than likely that individuals struggling and living from paycheck to paycheck, and or below the poverty level, do not have the luxury of an active gym membership or have the means to purchase exercise equipment. If you connect all the dots, you will begin to understand the numbers that show the poorest communities and people of color are getting really sick and dying in greater proportion. Let's face it—most people do not have the luxury of working in the security of their homes. Most people living below the poverty line are working on jobs that are now being deemed essential. So yes, this means they are working on the front lines of this pandemic, putting themselves at a greater risk of catching the virus and transmitting it to their loved ones. Now that certain jobs have been classified as 'essential', maybe it's time to give them essential pay.

Mandatory stay-at-home orders has really been rough on the entire country. We have multiple businesses being temporarily closed, millions of people without jobs. Something so minute and invisible has interrupted life as we know it. Every part of our lives has been impacted, and if you are one of the many people who are used to getting up on Sunday mornings, and going into the house of God to worship, then like millions of people all across the country, we have been forced to have church on line; although it's not the same as physically being in the house of God with other believers the presence and Word of God is as powerful as ever. I have been really enjoying Bishop Kim Brown and Pastor Deanneen Goodrich on Sunday mornings. The Word has been so refreshing that even though I am at home, I get up early enough to watch the 8 am service online. I find myself worshipping and praising God more now than ever. Don't get me wrong, I would love to be in the house of the Lord but my point is you can worship and praise God at any place, and at any time, if you are open to receive the presence of God. When the anointing is flowing, we should be able to move right into his presence, no matter where we are. The more time we spend in his presence on a regular basis, the easier it will be to enter in.

Nothing in the world will be able to stop our worship or the Word from going forward. The Word is still as sharp and powerful as it was before the pandemic, and it will continue to penetrate the heart and soul of man well after the pandemic. *Hebrews 4:12* says, "For the Word of God is living and active and full of power (making it operative), energizing, and effective). It is sharper than any two-edged sword, penetrating as far as the division of the soul and spirit (the completeness of a person), and of both joints and marrow (the deepest parts of our nature), exposing and judging the very thoughts and intentions of the heart."

Although we know that God did not cause this catastrophe, he is always in the center of every storm working on our behalf. We can get through this together if we continue to trust him, stay in his presence, obey and follow the guidelines from our leaders and the medical professionals. We know that there has to be something that we will learn from this, and that something good will come out of all of this. But we have to go through this process of life. We have never seen anything like this where one tragic event has impacted the entire world at the same time. I can only speculate the reason why this pandemic has come upon us in this season. But what I do know for sure is that I will take this time to further develop my relationship with Jesus Christ, and truly find out who he is to me and to the world.

Could it be possible that God allowed the very foundation of the body of believers to be turned upside down in order to get our attention? In previous chapters, if you recall, I touched on the subject of the distractions we face in our lives that enemy uses to take us farther and farther away from our true purpose. Sometimes we try so hard to please people instead of pleasing God that we miss the mark. We cannot allow people and things to come between the most essential relationship in our lives—yes, that would be the one with Jesus Christ. Could it be that true intimacy with him has to be restored? *Joel 2:12* says, "Even now," says the Lord, "Turn and come to Me with all your heart (in genuine repentance), With fasting and weeping and mourning (until every barrier is removed and the broken fellowship is restored)." Could it be that this season of isolation away from people is meant, as Bishop Kim Brown said in one of his sermons, to give us an opportunity to truly know Jesus as our Savior?

I recently came across a passage in *Jesus Calling Enjoying Peace in his Presence* by Sarah Young, that was so in sync with the season we currently find ourselves in. It said, "I am pleased by your tendency to turn to Me more and more frequently, especially when you are alone. When you are with other people, you often lose sight of My Presence. Your fear of displeasing people puts you in bondage to them, and they become your primary focus." We have been put into a position where we have no choice but to trust, lean on and depend on him. After this, some of us will truly know that he is our source and provider, our healer, our peace and joy, our protector, our way maker, our shelter, yes, ultimately our Savior. The season has arrived in which we can no longer put our trust in a business, in a job, and yes, even in the government. At some point in time, they will all be out of options but in spite of all of this he remains faithful, and he will continue to take care of our every need. *Proverbs 29:25* says, "The fear of man brings a snare, but whoever trusts in and puts his confidence in the Lord will be exalted and safe."

CHAPTER 16

The aftermath

According to Dictionary.com, 'giant' means "a person or thing of unusually great size, power, importance, etc.; major figure; legend: a giant in her field; an intellectual giant. Unusually large, great, or strong; gigantic; huge, greater or more eminent than others." Sounds like a perfect description of the church. A prime example of how things can go all so wrong when the giant is sleeping or distracted, is the battle between David and Goliath. *1 Samuel 17:4* describes Goliath as being a champion from the Philistines' camp, who was a giant nearly ten feet tall, and he was well-equipped for war. He was dressed in 126 pounds of armor, which included a bronze helmet, bronze shin guards. and a bronze sword. "His spear was like a fence rail—the spear tip alone weighed over fifteen pounds." It seemed he had everything he needed on the outside to win the battle but we all know the end of this story—he lost the battle and was killed and decapitated by someone who was so much smaller and weaker than him. I am fully aware that David had God on his side, so he was destined to win. But my point is that the giant fell asleep on the job by way of allowing the stature of his opponent to distract him and take him off of his game, and this along with him underestimating the strength that David had behind him, ended in him losing the battle and his life. It teaches us to never become so prideful that we underestimate our opponent. The church cannot underestimate the tricks and schemes of the enemy. We have to stay awake and stay focused on the tasked at hand.

We all hear the Word, read and study the Word but do we truly believe the Word? If we truly believe the Word of God then we should stand on that Word. We can pray all day long but we will continue to be ineffective and inefficient if we do not truly believe, receive and follow the Word of God when dealing with every aspect of our lives. Prayer is one of those weapons in our arsenal that we do not engage enough into the battle. If the leaders call for corporate prayer, be obedient and pray, and stop putting prayer on the back burner. By doing so, you are neglecting one of your most powerful weapons against the enemy. In this day and age, most churches are not praying enough. Some leaders will call for corporate prayer every once in a while, but corporate prayer should be held on a consistent basis, not just when you want God to bless your event or bail you out of a situation. The prayers are not just for the church's benefit— the prayers also have a huge impact on the world. *1 Peter 4:18* tells us, "And if the righteous scarcely be saved, where shall the ungodly and the sinner appear?"

The Church was built on a solid foundation by Christ over two thousand years ago to withstand everything in the enemy's arsenal; so, division, racism, religiosity, political discord, pride, false doctrine, inauthentic traditions, will not be able to come against his church. His church will stand in victory. *Ephesians 1:22-23*: "And He put all things (in every realm) in subjection under Christ's feet, and appointed Him as (supreme and authoritative) head over all things in the church, which is His body, the fullness of Him who fills and completes all things in all (believers). *Matthew 16:18* says, "And I say also unto thee, that thou art Peter, and upon this rock I will build my church; and the gates of hell shall not prevail against it." He gives his church the rights to his authority upon the earth in the form of binding and losing anything that is coming against us. *Matthew 16:19*: "And I will give unto thee the keys of the kingdom of heaven: and whatsoever thou shalt bind on earth shall be bound in heaven: and whatsoever thou shalt loose on earth shall be loosed in heaven."

The church was built on the foundation of the Word and faith. The last five years have been really challenging for the country, especially with all that has transpired in the world. I started this book talking about the impact of the 2016 election, and with much prayer, we would survive as a nation and get through all of the division and hate that has been resurrected since the election. Even though we are still in the midst of a political windstorm of dysfunction and division, we have to believe that we will survive and come out stronger than before. It is now 2020, and racism and hate are in the atmosphere like never before. Even in the midst of a pandemic, a young black man who was jogging, was shot dead by a white father and son duo. A young African American woman, named Breonna Taylor, was shot dead by police in her own bed. Our democracy and faith are under attack like never before. The church has to pull out every tool available in its arsenal to combat this cancer called 'hate' that is coming against our faith. We are almost four years in since the 2016 election, and we still face an uncertainty regarding healthcare.

I am trying to understand how individuals voted into office to protect the public are still making every attempt to dismantle and take away the healthcare in the middle of a pandemic. What do we do now as a country when millions of people already have or are at risk of losing their health insurance? This situation has made me a believer that this country needs to have some form of single payer system or a public option needs to be put in place ASAP—this is an emergency situation. People are dying without their loved ones being present. Allowing everyone to have insurance would give people a little comfort during these trying times. I have been praying that God will begin to put into office people after his own heart—leaders who are compassionate towards the needs of the people, leaders who revere him more than anything or anyone else. So yes, I have been praying consistently for this to change, and I will continue to pray for as long as it takes until one or two things happens—the heart of every lawmaker who is fighting against the well-being of the people changes and they see the light, or every lawmaker who continues to ignore the needs of the people is removed and replaced in Jesus' name.

God, we ask that you will assist your people in making wise and informative decisions, even when it comes to politics. And do not let us be fooled by the enemy but let us continue to seek you for direction in every circumstance. In the prior chapters, I mentioned some of the physical challenges that my family has faced over the past seven years, and I know and believe the Word but I also believe it is my right along with every other American to have and be able to afford quality healthcare. Do not get me wrong. I know that God is absolutely able to heal the sick instantly because I have seen him do some awesome things. I will continue to trust him as he makes a way for me to be whole even in the midst of this infirmity because his grace is sufficient for me. *2 Corinthians 12:8-9*: "Concerning this, I pleaded with the Lord three times that it might leave me; but He has said to me, 'My grace is sufficient for you (My loving kindness and My mercy are more than enough, always available regardless of the situation); for (My) power is being perfected (and is completed and shows itself most effectively) in (your) weakness." Therefore, I will all the more gladly boast in my weakness, so that the power of Christ (may dwell in me)."

We walk by faith and not by sight! Now let's dive back into humanitarianism. It is now 2020, and we are still in need of obtaining and developing more compassion for others. I realized this fact to be true when I saw a poll conducted by Pew Research Center that asked, if the US has a responsibility to accept refugees, and 68% of white Evangelicals said 'no' and 25% said 'yes', 50% of white mainline Protestants said 'no' and 43% said 'yes', 45% of Catholics said 'no' and 50% said 'yes', 31% of Religiously unaffiliated said 'no' and 65% said 'yes', 28% of black Protestants said 'no' and 63% said 'yes'. What is wrong with this picture when 65% of people that are not affiliated with the church have just as much or more compassion for people who are seeking refuge?

It's not hard to imagine what Jesus would do if he walked the earth today, and if you believe the Word of God, it's pretty clear that he would receive them with open arms. So, as the people of God, there should be no question as to what our answer should be. As I stated in one of the earlier chapters, I often pray that God will keep my heart full of love and compassion for others. Sometimes, we can become so bogged down with the things of this world and our own troubles that we cannot see past ourselves. So every now and then, we have to go back to the source and do some soul-searching to see if we are truly living in the will of God.

I would be remiss if I do not touch on one last topic before ending this chapter. And that would be the current moment we are living in right now, in which the world just witnessed the horrific death of another black man, Mr. George Floyd, on video. Prior to watching Mr. Floyd's murder on video, I truly thought that nothing else regarding racism and police brutality could shock me but of course, after watching three officers holding Mr. Floyd down, with one of the officers burying his knee into Mr. Floyd's neck for more than eight minutes, in spite of the pleas and cries of "I can't breathe" from Mr. Floyd who was obviously in distress was truly shocking. His cry for help was ignored for almost six minutes until he became unconscious, and to add insult to injury, even after Mr. Floyd became unconscious, the officer's knee remained buried into his neck for another three minutes and twenty-nine seconds. The image and the sound of Mr. Floyd slowly dying along with the image of the nonchalant officer with his hands in his pockets and knee buried in the back of Mr. Floyd's neck will forever be ingrained in my mind. The morning after viewing that horrific video, I woke up with such a heavy heart, so much so that I really had to worship my way out of the state that I woke up in. I had to pull from that source within, yes, I am referring to that Hope of Glory that resides within every believer. I had to tap into that source before I could even place my feet on the floor to start my day.

As a country, we have witnessed many injustices but it was just something about seeing this tragic death that really shook me. So, I really had to dig deep and cry out to the living God from the depths of my soul to obtain some type of relief from this pain in my heart. "My soul longeth, yea, even fainteth for the courts of the Lord: my heart and my flesh crieth out for the living God.": *Psalms 84:2*. I was totally honest when I went to God in prayer about my feelings of pain, fear and anger regarding the continuing injustices perpetrated against people of color. I don't believe the Creator of the universe created me as a person of color to be looked upon as less than, bad or inferior to others because of the color of my skin. This hypothesis is totally contrary to the Word of God because we all know, according to his Word, we were all made in his image. *Genesis 1:27* says, "So God created man in his own image; in the image of God, he created him; male and female he created them." *Ephesians 2:10* says, "For we are his workmanship, created in Christ Jesus unto good works, which God hath before ordained that we should walk in them."

It is so critical in this moment and time that the body of Christ stand up and be unified against this ancient demonic force name racism, and to my white evangelical sisters and brothers, you can no longer remain silent. Remaining silent can be looked upon as being complicit. We have to work together as one body to crush this evil that has plagued our nation for many centuries. We have to have the mindset that enough is enough. It's time for the reign of racism to end as we know it. As the body of Christ, we have the power to do it together but it starts with us presenting as one unified body. If you say you love me with the love of Christ, then Speak up for what is right! *Proverbs 31:8-9* says, "Open your mouth for the mute, For the rights of all who are unfortunate and defenseless; Open your mouth, judge righteously, and administer justice for the afflicted and needy."

"Am I my brother's keeper?" Everybody knows the story in the Bible about Cain and Abel. After Cain killed his brother out of jealousy, God caught up with him and asked, where is your brother Abel? Cain said to God, "Am I my brother's keeper"? If you are a part of the body of Christ, the answer is yes you are. As I discussed in a previous chapter, just like the human body, every organ in the body supports another, so the same is required of the body of Christ. It works both ways, as one body, we are supposed to support one another. So are we really doing everything we can to support each other? Once again, we cannot be fooled into thinking all is well in my life so God has to be pleased with me. We all sometimes, have to take the time to self-reflect and go to God in prayer, asking him to help us to objectively see ourselves through the lens of his Spirit. It is critical in the times that we are living in that we continually return to the source for clarity and restoration. *Genesis 4:9-11* says, "Then the Lord said to Cain, 'Where is Abel your brother?' And he (lied and) said, 'I do not know. Am I my brother's keeper?' The Lord said, 'What have you done? The voice of your brother's (innocent) blood is crying out to Me from the ground (for justice)'."

As a people, we have been crying out to God for justice since the start of slavery, and we will continue to cry out until he pours out his justice upon the earth and removes all shackles. I would like to tell you about an interesting conversation that I had with one of my white Evangelical brothers in Christ. I finally have some understanding as to why 80% of white Evangelicals supported the current administration during the 2016 election. Some of them felt that Donald Trump could deliver for them—deliver religious freedoms, judges who would help them fight their causes. The gentleman I spoke to enlightened me to the fact that a couple of days before the election, they came together, got down on their knees to pray, and because of their prayers, they believe that God turned it around for their candidate. He also said, "We got back on our knees a second time to pray for forgiveness because if this is who God has chosen to lead us instead of given us a king like Hezekiah," he jokingly added, "this is who he believes we are worthy to receive to lead us." We discussed a variety of issues including policing, and how I believed that since the 2016 election, the country is more divided as ever. He seemed not to be aware of the divide. I believe since we come from different cultures, backgrounds and experiences, our outlook on the world would be different. He then asked me if I saw where the black unemployment rate was at the lowest that it has ever been before the pandemic, and if I had any insight on that fact. I told him if those numbers were including the two or three low-paying jobs that most people were working to make ends meet, then the answer would be 'yes'. The income inequality between blacks and whites is appalling. He proceeded to tell me that he did not grow up around black people, and his first time meeting a person of color was when he went into the military. After he shared that part of his life, it suddenly became crystal clear, that he may never totally understand the trials and tribulations of an oppressed people because he has never had to walk in the shoes of those that have been oppressed and have been living in a methodical bondage for over four hundred years.

We may not always be able to relate to each other's experiences and pain but as fellow Christians, because of the love of Christ that we all share as Christians, we should be able to empathize and share in each other's pain. I came to the conclusion that all those who have not been able to relate to this moment in time and deal with the hard truth of this country's darkness have to be enlightened by and willing to see and receive the truth. But until that happens, they will continue to live in that bubble of blindness. I will continue to pray that God will open our eyes and allow us to see clearly through his spiritual eyes in Jesus' name.

In conclusion, as the body of Christ, we have to know and believe what the Word says about his church. We are the head and not the tail, above and not beneath, lenders and not borrowers, a royal priesthood, the salt of the earth… The church should be moving in sync with the Word of God, living in his magnificent glory; not living a defeated, oppressed and depressed life but a blessed life. We are a glorious church full of our Father's majesty and power. So awake old, sleeping giant! Arise, and shine, take your rightful place. The victory is yours in Jesus' name. The deal has already been brokered on the cross with the blood of Jesus, and we have won. Hallelujah, we've won!

Ephesians 5:27: "That he might present it to himself a glorious church, not having spot, or wrinkle, or any such thing; but that it should be holy and without blemish." *Revelations 21:4:* "He will wipe away every tear from their eyes. There will be no more death or mourning or crying or pain, for the old order of things has passed away."